UNIVERSITY OF NORTH CAROLINA
STUDIES IN THE ROMANCE LANGUAGES AND LITERATURES
Number 131

I0660971

THE ORIGINS OF THE BAROQUE CONCEPT
OF *PEREGRINATIO*

THE ORIGINS OF THE
BAROQUE CONCEPT
OF *PEREGRINATIO*

BY

JUERGEN HAHN

CHAPEL HILL

THE UNIVERSITY OF NORTH CAROLINA PRESS

DEPÓSITO LEGAL: V. 1.678 - 1973

ARTES GRÁFICAS SOLER, S. A. - JÁVEA, 28 - VALENCIA (8) - 1973

CONTENTS

TO MY PARENTS

PREFACE

The factors which influenced the development of this study are complex. The topic underwent its first scholarly rehearsal in the form of a doctoral dissertation presented at Duke University. This was, in a sense, the product of a long-nurtured interest in a particular literary period, an interest which had probably been awakened during the undergraduate days at the University of Michigan, where the late Professor Edward Glaser delivered his enthusiastic lectures on Cervantes. The actual composition of the study benefitted from much helpful advice gleaned from conversations with members of Duke's Department of Romance Languages, and with Professor Edmund Reiss from the English Department. The discerning editorship of Professor Juan B. Avalle-Arce enhanced the present revision. And special appreciation is accorded to Professor Bruce W. Wardropper, whose devoted graduate coaching and whose untiring and enlightened guidance of the original dissertation project were exemplary.

We readily concede that in a study such as the present one completeness is difficult to achieve. Moreover what some readers may miss, others would rather see omitted for the sake of conciseness. For example, the question of the adequacy of the term "baroque" would have seemed to merit a thorough theoretical discussion. We find, however, that a different generation of scholars already has, through dedicated labor and spirited controversy, dignified the term and rendered it largely acceptable. The written results of their worthy efforts are readily accessible to the interested reader. For omissions of this kind, therefore, we ask not indulgence but understanding.

One note about translations. These were provided simply to enhance understanding and readability. In certain cases authoritative translations were consulted, though these were generally found to be adaptable in only a limited way to the special aims of this study, which are clarification and verbal accuracy. Therefore unless otherwise stated, we assume responsibility for all of them. Translations of Biblical quotations are those of the King James version.

J. H.

Berkeley, 1972

ABBREVIATIONS OF REFERENCES

BAE	*Biblioteca de Autores Españoles*
BSS	*Bulletin of Spanish Studies*
MP	*Modern Philology*
NBAE	*Nueva Biblioteca de Autores Españoles*
NRFH	*Nueva Revista de Filología Hispánica*
PG	Migne, *Patrologiae cursus completus. Series graeca.*
PL	Migne, *Patrologiae cursus completus. Series latina.*
PMLA	*Publications of the Modern Language Association*
RFH	*Revista de Filología Hispánica*
SP	*Studies in Philology*

INTRODUCTION

The theme of wandering, alienation, and exile, combined with that of pious devotion, is omnipresent in the Spanish literature of the Golden Age. It is subsumed in the word *peregrinación*. Antonio Vilanova, who has devoted two studies to this theme, has concluded that it permeates not only Spanish literature but Italian and Portuguese literature as well.[1] Our own study is not entended to rehearse the findings of Vilanova, but to complement them in a manner which we shall explain in the appropriate chapters.[2]

The term *peregrinación* as used in the baroque age is complex. The nature of this complexity is illustrated by a poem by the seventeenth-century writer Bartolomé Cairasco de Figueroa, entitled "Peregrinación":

> No es Peregrinación aquel vagante,
> Inquieto y solícito camino
> Del que por ser curioso es caminante,
>   Ni el que por melancólico destino
> O por necesidad o vanagloria,
> O por intento vano es peregrino.
>   La peregrinación que de memoria
> Y de alabanza es digna en cielo y suelo,
> Y la que se encarece en esta historia,
>   Es la de aquel que con piadoso celo,
> Por voluntad u obligación, visita

---

[1] "El peregrino andante en el *Persiles* de Cervantes," *Boletín de la Real Academia de buenas letras de Barcelona*, XXII (1949), 97-159. Also "El peregrino de amor en las *Soledades* de Góngora," *Estudios Dedicados a Menéndez Pidal* (Madrid, 1952), III, 421-460.

[2] See our Chapters II and III.

Los lugares que acá señala el cielo,
  Y cuando algún rigor le necesita
A padecer trabajos y fatigas,
Como Faustino padeció y Jovita,
  Entonces va cogiendo las espigas,
Y los ricos manojos, con que vuelve,
Triunfando de las armas enemigas.
  La peregrinación santa resuelve
Las postemas del alma y las deshace,
Y el cuerpo lo de dentro afuera vuelve.
  La indómita cerviz que al mundo aplace
De la rebelde carne rinde y doma
Si con debida devoción se hace.
  Es peregrinación blanca paloma
Que por hallar descanso gime y vuela
Por Compostela, Palestina y Roma;
  Es un peregrinar en la vihuela
Con pasos y con fugas inauditas,
Que el ánimo y el ánima consuela;
  Es un andar buscando margaritas
Y darlas por la gracia del que adoro,
A cuyo amor van todas sobrescritas;
  Es hallar en el campo un gran tesoro,
Y sacar a vender lo nuevo y viejo
De su caudal quien tiene plata y oro;
  Y en fin, es ver quien somos al espejo,
Pues somos peregrinos y estranjeros
Hasta pasar triunfando el mar Bermejo. [3]

A pilgrimage is not that straying, restless, anxious
walk of the traveler [travelling] out of curiosity,
  Nor is he a pilgrim who wanders out of necessity or
pride or vainglory.
  The pilgrimage which is worthy of remembrance and
praise in Heaven and on earth, and which is being exalted
in this story
  Is the one which is directed by pious zeal, by choice
or obligation to those places which Heaven has pointed
out down here.
  And when adversity compels him [i.e., the pilgrim]
to suffer hardships and exhaustion as [it compelled] Faustino and Jovita,

---

[3] BAE, XLII, 466. The poem, obviously an introduction to a hagio-
graphical work, is included in a nineteenth-century anthology of "Defini-
ciones poéticas, morales y cristianas," culled from Cairasco's writings.

He will then gather the spikes; and the plentiful bundle which he brings back [will allow him] to triumph over the arms of the enemy.

The holy pilgrimage cures the sores of the soul and dissolves them, and the body turns out what is inside of it.

The indomitable neck of the rebellious flesh which takes pleasure in the world [the pilgrimage] subdues and tames, if it is performed with due devotion.

A pilgrimage is a white dove which for want of rest moans and flies toward Santiago de Compostela, Palestine and Rome.

It is a pilgrimage [of the fingers] over the [strings of a] guitar, with its paces and unheard-of fugues that console mind and spirit.

It is a search for daisies, their presentation to the one that I adore, and to whose love they are addressed.

It is finding a large treasure in the land and someone's offering for sale the new and the old by him who possesses silver and gold.

And finally it is to see in the mirror who we are, since we are strangers and pilgrims until we triumphantly cross the Red Sea.

Cairasco, taking vehement issue with what he considers the improper use of the word, sets out to rectify it. In the main he rejects the use of the term as meaning a general sense of wandering, a straying and loitering which betrays a restless spirit or an obsession with a personal problem. Rather, he asserts, the most appropriate meaning is that of the devotional pilgrimage to the shrine of a saint, undertaken for the purpose of penitence. He also emphasizes the Biblical usage of the term by drawing an analogy between the pilgrimage of life which is undertaken by all mankind and the exodus of the Israelites. The latter two meanings, being profoundly Christian, are those to which Cairasco would restrict the term.

This diversity of meaning is also shared by the other Romance cognates of the term because of their common descent from the Latin *peregrinatio.* Thus we have in French *pèlerinage* and *pérégrination,* and in Italian *pellegrinaggio* and *peregrinazione.* [4] The

---

[4] The Romance languages tended to develop two kinds of etymologies of the word, one popular and one learned. Thus Fr. *pèlerinage,* It. *pel-*

English words *pilgrimage* and *peregrination* likewise betray their Romance or Latin origin, as does the German *Pilgerschaft*. For the sake of unity and consistency, then, we shall henceforth employ the Latin word *peregrinatio* except in direct quotations.

The opposition between the Christian and the non-Christian meaning of the term *peregrinatio* on which Cairasco insists is not limited to the baroque. It is as old as Christianity. In order to trace the origin of this opposition we must therefore step back into antiquity and investigate the special nature of the term and the reason for its adoption by Christian thought.

The two terms which are of greatest importance in our investigation of the ancient sources are, on the one hand, the Greek ξενιτεία which derives from ξένος and, on the other, the Latin *peregrinatio* which derives from *peregrinus*. As to the Latin terms, the primary reason for choosing them for our investigation is their semantic inclusiveness, as well as their wide applicability in the form of their Romance derivatives. Thus the term *itinerarium*, which during the Middle Ages often denoted a devotional pilgrimage, does not include the status of the stranger. *Hospes*, 'stranger' may not refer to the devotional pilgrim. This limitation also applies to *alienus*. The word *viator* was not readily rendered into the vernacular. *Romaeus*, which corresponds closely to *peregrinus* and which also occurs in the Romance vernaculars, does not occur in Classical Latin, nor did it have quite as broad an impact as *peregrinus*. [5] The advantages of focusing our attention

---

legrinaggio, and Sp. *peregrinaje* represent the popular development. In some vernaculars the popular version is more current than others. Thus Fr. *pèlerinage* is still widely used whereas Sp. *peregrinaje* is far less current than *peregrinación*. The change from medial *-r-* to *-l-* which appears in some vernaculars is attested by Wartburg as having taken place in the Vulgar Latin period. (See *Französisches etymologisches Wörterbuch,* s.v. *peregrinus.*) On the other hand Fr. *pérégrination,* It. *peregrinazione,* Sp. *peregrinación* betray the recent borrowing from Latin through learned influence.

[5] Dante in fact differentiated between *pellegrino* and *romeo*: the former was a pilgrim to Santiago whereas the latter was a pilgrim to Rome. On the other hand, a *palmiero* was a pilgrim to the Holy Land:

> E però è da sapere, che in tre modi si chiamano propriamente le genti che vanno al servigio dell' Altissimo; chiamansi *palmieri,* in quanto vanno oltremare, là onde molte volte recano la palma; chiamansi *pellegrini,* in quanto vanno alla Casa de Gallizia, perocchè la sepoltura di S. Jacopo fu più lontano dalla sua patria, che

on *peregrinus* and its derivatives are apparent. In this study we shall therefore limit ourselves almost exclusively to this term. There is also a great practical advantage in keeping the terminology constant, because it is against a uniform background that the enormous variety of applications which the concept experienced in the course of history will be more readily perceived.

The Latin words *peregrinus, peregrinatio, peregrinari* originate from the roots *per* — 'through' and — *ager* 'field.' The *peregrinus* thus was one who traversed the countryside. Once the wanderer left his home country he became a stranger wherever he went. So *peregrinus* came to be synonymous with 'stranger' and 'foreigner.' In the Roman empire this term denoted 'alien,' that is, one who did not possess the citizenship of Rome. Roman citizenship was for a long time restricted to a minority of the empire's population, and it was only this minority which enjoyed all the benefits of the *ius civile*, the civil law. [6] The remaining population did not share these advantages; although they were indigenous, they lived in a sense as strangers in their own country. It was not until 212 A.D., when the emperor Caracalla extended Roman citizenship to all subjects, that the status of the *peregrinus* was relinquished within the Empire.

This development of the meaning of *peregrinus* is perhaps the most striking indication of the precarious condition which

---

di alcuno altro Apostolo; chiamansi *romei,* in quanto vanno a Roma, là ove questi, che io chiamo pellegrini, andavano.

And it must be realized that the people who go into the service of the Highest are actually named in three [different] ways: they are called *palmieri* if they go overseas [to the Holy Land], from where they often bring back the palm [-branch as evidence of their arrival there]; they are called *pellegrini* if they go to the [Holy] House of Galicia, because the sepulcher of Santiago was further away than that of any other Apostle; they are called *romei* if they go to Rome, where those whom I call "pellegrini" used to go.

(Cited from Niccolò Tommaseo and Bernardo Bellini, *Dizionario della lingua italiana,* s.v. *pellegrinc.*) Leo Spitzer has shown that Dante's etymology is erroneous. The appellation *romaeus* stems from the fact that the pilgrims to the Holy Land had to traverse the Byzantine Empire, which during the Middle Ages was still known as Rome. See "Aprov. *romęu,* ital. *romęo,* afrz. *romier,* 'Pilger'," *ZRPh,* LVI (1936), 644-645.

[6] See Pauly-Wissowa, *Realencyclopädie der classischen Altertumswissenschaft,* s.v. *peregrinus.*

is potentially the stranger's lot everywhere and at all times. Not only is the stranger naturally disadvantaged because of his lack of familiarity with the foreign country, but this dilemma may be aggravated by the legal disadvantages imposed on him. It is not surprising that the man of antiquity should be highly preoccupied with the status of the stranger to the extent of seeing in him the stuff of human drama, worthy to be portrayed in prominent works of literature. Such, for example, is the case in Greek literature. In Greece the term for stranger and foreigner, ξένος, became a legal term as it did in Rome. [7] The ξένος too was the non-citizen. However, there was never a uniform Greek citizenship for the whole country as there was eventually for all the Roman empire. In Greece each city had its own citizenship. Thus, whenever one left the immediate vicinity of the city, one lived as a foreigner, exposed to all the hazards of that status.

Perhaps the most prominent literary example, if not the archetype, of the stranger and his dilemma is Ulysses. Not only is he exposed to all the hazards of his errant sea-voyage, but he is also forced to live with foreign people, all of whom may be, and often are, hostile. Lacking the rights of citizenship, he is dependent for his well-being in their good will. This becomes evident in the scene in which Ulysses is found shipwrecked by Nausicaa. Upon seeing him, she beckons the women of her entourage to attend to him:

> ἀλλ' ὅδε τις δύστηνος ἀλώμενος ἐνθάδ᾽ ἱκάνει,
> τὸν νῦν χρὴ κομέειν. πρὸς γὰρ Διός εἰσιν ἅπαντες
> ξεῖνοί τε πτωχοί τε, δόσις δ᾽ ὀλίγη τε φίλη τε.
> ἀλλὰ δότ᾽, ἀμφίπολοι, ξείνῳ βρῶσίν τε πόσιν τε.[8]

This is an unfortunate wanderer that has come here. We must tend to him; for from Zeus are all strangers and beggars, and a gift, though small, is welcome. Come, my maidens, give to the stranger food and drink.

Nausicaa is ready to give aid to the ξένος because such hospitality amounts to a gesture of devotion to Zeus. Zeus has a special af-

---

[7] See Pauly-Wissowa, s.v. ξενίας γραφή.
[8] Homer, *The Odyssey*, ed. and trans. A. T. Murray (London, 1930), Bk. VI, vv. 206-208.

fection for the ξένος and regards him as his protégé. Ulysses in a way functions as a touchstone to test men's readiness to do obeissance to Zeus by assisting the god's favorite; and the *Odyssey* as a whole represents a test case of the human relationships between the stranger and his surrounding fellow men. Throughout the poem the good are distinguished from the evil ones by their hospitality and solicitude for the stranger. Poliphemus, for example, violates the sacred laws of hospitality by his intention to kill the strangers; and the suitors at Ithaca, rather than attending to the needs of the ξένος make a sport of him.

The function of Zeus as the protector of the stranger is also stressed in Aeschylus' play *The Supplicants*. Here fifty women who had fled their homeland to avoid having to marry their fifty cousins entreat Zeus to safeguard them:

ἄγε δὴ λέξωμεν ἐπ' 'Αργείοις
εὐχὰς ἀγαθὰς ἀγαθῶν ποινάς
Ζεὺς δ'ἐφορεύοι ξένιος ξενίου
στόματος τιμὰς επ'ἀληθείᾳ,
τέρμον' ἀμέμτους πρὸς ἄπαντα.[9]

Let us then say a prayer for the people of Argos to effect blessings. And may Zeus who guards strangers grant fulfillment to the entreaties of the strangers whose desire is limitless.

When they ask King Pelasgos for asylum, he hesitates momentarily because he fears retaliation from the fifty cousins. But eventually he obtains the permission from his assembly, because he does not want to offend Zeus.

Kindness to strangers, then, was an important part of the pagan thought of antiquity. It was mandatory because the godhead himself championed the stranger's cause.

The Christian God, too, regards the stranger as his protégé. [10] Moreover, through Christ's incarnation God took upon himself the condition of the ξένος:

---

[9] Aischylos, *Die Schutzsuchenden,* ed. Walther Kraus (Frankfurt, 1948), ll. 625ff.

[10]   [Deus] facit iudicium pupillo et viduae, amat peregrinum et dat ei victum atque vestitum. Et vos ergo amate peregrinos, quia et ipsi fuistis advenae in terra Aegypti (Deut. 10, 18-19).

'Επείνασα γὰρ καὶ ἐδώκατέ μοι φαγεῖν, ἐδίψασα καὶ ἐποτίσατέ με, ξένος ἤμην καὶ συνηγάγετέ με. [11]

For I was an hungered, and ye gave me meat: I was thirsty and ye gave me drink: I was a stranger, and ye took me in.

Here we note the decisive difference between the pagan and the Christian concept of the stranger's lot. Zeus only protects the stranger. He does not himself become one. Christ not only protects, but identifies himself with the stranger in a gesture of unprecedented solidarity. Because of Christ's action the preoccupation with the stranger is central to Christian thought. Christianity is the religion of the stranger and the outsider, of the disadvantaged and the oppressed. In addition, Christian thought compares life on earth with the condition of the stranger. For the Christian, then, the concept of *peregrinatio* comprises a constellation of meanings. Whenever he has occasion to be a stranger — for example by traveling abroad — he associated his own condition with these literal and metaphorical meanings. Some of the important consequences which arose from this association of ideas will constitute the topic of our first chapter.

[God] doth execute the judgment of the fatherless and widow, and loveth the stranger, in giving him food and raiment. Love ye therefore the stranger; for ye were strangers in the land of Egypt.

[11] Matth. 25, 35. The Vulgate translates ξένος as *hospes* in this case. Although normally I quote from the Vulgate, I here give the Greek version to demonstrate that the Christian term partakes of the cultural heritage of the pagan one. In the Vulgate Christ is identified in Luke 24, 18 as *peregrinus*. See our Chapter III.

CHAPTER I

THE VOYAGE OF DISCOVERY IN LITERATURE

PEREGRINATIO: *The Voyage into the Unknown*

In a passage in Camões' *Os Lusíadas* (1572) the seafarer and explorer Vasco da Gama, having barely escaped with his ships and crew from the treachery of the Moors, thanks Divine Providence and invokes its continued protection:

> E se te move tanto a piedade
> D'esta mísera gente peregrina,
> Que so por tua altíssima bondade
> Da gente a salvas, pérfida e malina,
> Nalgum pôrto seguro de verdade
> Conduzir-nos já agora determina,
> Ou nos amostra a terra, que buscamos;
> Pois so por teu serviço navegamos. [1]

And if pity for this wretched wandering people moved You to save us, out of Your supreme goodness alone, from treacherous and evil enemies, then lead us now to some truly safe harbor; or reveal to us the land we seek, since it is in Your service that we sail.

A tone of self-pity pervades the stanza. The Portuguese on their perilous voyage to India stop over at Mombassa in the hope of finding friendly people there, perhaps even Christians with whom

---

[1] Luis de Camões, *Os Lusíadas*, ed. J. D. M. Ford, in *Harvard Studies in Romance Languages*, XXII (Cambridge, Mass., 1946), Canto II, v. 32.

they can establish relations. Instead, the insidious Moors prepare a trap and da Gama and his men are saved only through the timely intervention of Venus. It is an extremely disheartening experience for them, because after weeks of battling the sea and travelling on an uncertain course in an unknown part of the world, even the longed-for port offers no respite and instead threatens them with danger:

> No mar tanta tormenta, e tanto dano!
> Tantas vezes a morte apercibida!
> Na terra tanta guerra, tanto engano,
> Tanta necessidade avorrecida!
> Onde pode acolher-se um fraco humano?
> Onde terá segura a curta vida? (I, 106)

> On sea [there is] so much upheaval and so much havoc, and the specter of death often so close. On land [there is] so much hostility and deception, so much hateful deprivation. Where can a frail human being find refuge? Where can he live his brief life securely?

Summing up their plight they label themselves "mísera gente peregrina," a wandering people worthy of compassion. Being far from home and deprived of a resting place, they are forced to continue their wandering about and their suffering, a condition that is a most appropriate illustration of life in general:

> Ó grandes e gravíssimos perigos!
> Ó caminho da vida nunca certo!
> Que aonde a gente poem sua esperança,
> Tenha a vida tam pouca segurança. (I, 105)

> How great and grievous the dangers are! How uncertain the path of life! Wherever people may place their hopes, they will find little security in life.

Yet in spite of this suffering the recurring theme of the poem is the insistence that they must push on into the unknown regions, "por mares nunca de antes navegados" (I, 1). It is a sense of mission which impels them to venture forth and accept the sacrifices. When asked what brought them to the Orient, da Gama replies that it is his mission of spreading Christianity:

Abrindo, lhe responde, o mar profundo,
Por onde nunca veio gente humana,
Vimos buscar do Indo a gram corrente,
Por onde a lei divina se acrecente. (VII, 25).

"We came," he answered, "to explore the high seas, where no humans sailed before, and to find the mighty current of the Indus, so that [through our mission] the Divine cause may be enhanced."

The Missionary and the Journey into the Unknow

Such missionary zeal was not uncommon among the Renaissance voyagers; together with the desire to seek trade or conquer the riches of the Orient it constituted a dominant motive for their voyages. Columbus too evalutes his discovery of the New World as a spiritual as well as a material gain:

...gócese Cristo en la tierra cual se regocija en los Cielos, al ver la próxima salvación de tantos pueblos, entregados hasta ahora a la perdición. Regocijémonos, así por la exaltación de nuestra fe como por el aumento de bienes temporales, de los cuales no sólo habrá de participar la España sino toda la Cristiandad. [2]

...may Christ rejoice on earth as he does in Heaven, at the sight of the immanent salvation of so many people who until now had been destined to doom. Let us rejoice at the uplifting of our faith as well as at the increase in worldly riches in which not only Spain but the whole of Christianity will share.

Magellan too will die in the defense of a newly converted tribe in Indonesia, thus characterizing the strong sense of mission that impelled these early and principal discoverers. It was a sense of mission accompanied by the desire of possession without being overshadowed by it.

Such motivation could not arise without precedents, and it is a commonplace of historians to point to the missionary zeal

---

[2] *Cartas de relación de la conquista de América,* ed. Julio Le Reverend (Mexico, 1945), I, 32.

in order to point out the strikingly medieval outlook of these seafarers. [3] The proselytizing of unbelievers had been the supreme task of the Church since its beginnings, and the distances to be covered were no hindrance to the self-sacrificing missionaries. Nestorian missionaries are attested to have travelled as far as China as early as the ninth century, successfully converting large numbers of natives. [4] In 845, however, a disastrous persecution removed nearly all traces of their labors, and it was not until the twelfth century that the activity was renewed, this time not by the heretical Nestorians but by official papal emissaries and missionaries whose aim was to convert as well as to establish relations with the Mongol rulers who were attacking Islam from the east. [5]

These missionaries undertook their task with ascetic zeal. One such man, Odric de Fore Julii, composed in 1330 *Le Livre des merveilles du monde* in which he characterizes his mission in the following manner:

> Cy commence le chemin de la pérégrination et du voiage que fist un bon homme de l'Ordre des frères meneurs, nommé frère Odric de Fore Julii ... qui par le commant du Pappe ala oultre mer pour preschier aux mescréants la foy de Dieu. [6]

> Here begins the pilgrimage and voyage which a gentleman of the Ordre des Frères Mineurs, by the name of Friar Odric de Fore Julii, undertook ... who by the order of the Pope went abroad to preach the faith of God to the infidels.

He calls his trip a "pérégrination et voiage" to call attention to its dual aspect. Since the actual purpose of his book is to relate

---

[3] H. V. Livermore, A *History of Portugal* (Cambridge, Mass., 1947), pp. 185-192. Commerce, missionary activity and the search for the mythical Prester John motivated the voyagers of Henry the Navigator, according to the chronicler Azurara.

[4] Paul Herrmann, *Conquest by Man* (London, 1954), pp. 343-349.

[5] Herrmann, p. 348.

[6] *Le Livre des merveilles du monde*, in *L'Extrême Orient au Moyen Age*, ed. Louis de Backer (Paris, 1877), p. 89. This old French version is a translation from the original Latin, done by Jean le Lonc in 1351.

the "merveilles du monde" in travelog form, he calls his trip a
voiage, i.e., a secular journey. Since it goes *oultre mer*, it goes
beyond the known confines of the European world and is therefore,
by its simple appeal to curiosity, worthy of being transmitted to
interested readers. In the Middle Ages, however, such journeys
were not normally undertaken for their own sake or for pleasure,
least of all by official members of the Church. For the Church
would tend to downgrade the intrinsic value of travel, as did
Thomas à Kempis, for example, in that widely read prescription
for asceticism, *De imitatione Christi* (ca. 1413):

> Quid potes alibi videre, quod hic non videas? Ecce coe-
> lum & terram & omnia elementa: nam ex istis omnia sunt
> facta. Quid potes alicubi videre, quod diu potest sub
> sole permanere? [7]

> What can you see elsewhere that you cannot see here?
> Behold the sky, the earth, and all the elements, for of
> these are all things made. What can you see anywhere
> else, which can endure for long?

Since the whole of the world is the result of God's creative effort,
the contemplation of one part of his creation at one's home is
sufficient to impart an idea of the whole. Within the scope of
such a *Weltanschauung* travel could not logically edify the soul;
indeed it could harm it if it were meant only for the indulgence
of the senses:

> Trahunt desideria sensualitatis ad spatiandum: sed cum
> hora transierit, quid nisi gravitatem conscientiae, & cordis
> dispersionem reportas? [8]

> The desire of the senses compels you to roam about, but
> when their hour is spent, what do you bring back but a
> burdened conscience and a distracted heart?

---

[7] Thomas à Kempis, *De Imitatione Christi libri quattuor*, ed. J. Valart
(Paris, 1773), Bk. I, Ch. 20.

[8] Kempis, I, 20.

To avoid compromising himself, therefore, the devout Christian would ideally travel only for a lofty purpose. [9] The most appropriate type of travel was the pilgrimage to the shrine of a saint or even to the Holy Land. These had taken place ever since the origin of Christianity, but it was not until the year 1000 that large numbers of people made their way to the Holy Land in expectation of the Millenium. So numerous were the pilgrimages undertaken by the devotees that the term for travel became synonymous for "pilgrimage." [10] Its meaning thus became more inclusive, because now it embraced the idea of travel as well as its devotionary purpose. The *peregrinatio* of the missionary, though it is not a pilgrimage, has nevertheless a devotionary, a spiritual end, namely the extension of Christendom for the greater glory of God.

This idea is yet further developed in the travelog of another missionary, the *Relation du voiage de frère Bieul,* written by Friar Bieul who also sets out to the Orient. Bieul states that he travels with an apostolic mission, "pour aler ès tesmoignage de Dieu." He then proceeds to expound the ascetic nature of his trip:

---

[9] This did not, of course, prevent all manner of secular travel from being performed with increasing frequency as the Middle Ages advanced, as is pointed out, for example, by F. R. H. Du-Boulay in *An Age of Ambition: English Society in the Late Middle Ages* (New York, 1970), Ch. I. We might ask, however, to what extent the idea of secular travel could strike a chord in the medieval mind and inspire it to spiritual contemplation. The concept of *peregrinatio* implies the presence of at least a potential for spiritual preoccupation, which is readily observed, for instance, in medieval descriptions of knight-errantry and knighthood, which were indeed eventually associated with *peregrinatio* (see our Chapter III). However, such a spiritual potential could not as readily be attributed to the activities of traveling merchants, journeymen, goliards, or students. The *Travels of Marco Polo,* for example, reveal little spiritual concern. Since this book also paid little homage to official Christendom's religiously inspired geographic fictions, it found surprisingly little resonance among his immediate contemporaries. (See Henry H. Hart, *Venetian Adventurer: Marco Polo* [Stanford, 1942], p. 257.) On the other hand, the *Peregrinatio Sancti Brendani* not only respects but exalts Christian legends. Its lasting popularity during a considerable part of the Middle Ages is attested by its appearance in a variety of Western European languages.

[10] W. Wartburg, *Französisches etymologisches Wörterbuch,* s.v. *peregrinus.*

> Lors repensay en mon courage que point ne me seroit
> seur de longuement estre oiseux, sans essaier et esprouver
> aucune chose de labour et de pouvreté de lonc voiage et
> de pérégrinacions. [11]

> So I reflected in my heart that I would not be assured
> for long [of my patience] to remain idle without trying
> and experiencing some of the hardships and deprivations
> of long journeys and peregrinations.

The idea of becoming a missionary had come to him when he
considered the benefits he derived from Christ and the fact that
Christ himself had made a *peregrinatio* on this earth:

> Dieu ... envoya son seul filx Dieu Jhesucrist faire sa
> pérégrinacion en ce monde e mourir pour nous pécheurs.

> God ... sent His only[-begotten] son Jesus Christ to per-
> form His pilgrimage in this world and to die for us
> sinners.

He suggests thereby that he considers his own *peregrinatio* an
imitation of Christ's, namely to save souls from perdition. [12] Evidently his comparison had widespread validity because the
seventeenth-century chronicler Samual Purchas also speaks of
"Christ's Pilgrimage in the flesh to recover him (man)." [13] Likewise
he speaks of the "Apostles' Peregrinations" when he refers to
their missionary travels, a notion which likewise compares with
a medieval source, the liturgical plays in which the apostles are
named *peregrini*. [14]

With Christ and the Apostles as prototypes the medieval missionary possessed ample precedents on which to model his task.
He could, moreover, reflect that life itself was for the Christian
a *peregrinatio*, a wandering in exile from the Heavenly abode.

---

[11] *Relation du voyage du frère Bieul*, in *L'Extreme Orient au Moyen Age*, ed. Louis de Backer (Paris, 1877), p. 257. This old French version is a translation from the original Latin, performed by Jean le Lonc.

[12] *Relation du voyage du frère Bieul*, p. 257. See also our Chapter III.

[13] Samuel Purchas, *Purchas His Pilgrimes* (Glasgow, 1905), I, 135.

[14] Otto Schüttpelz, "Die Erscheinungen vor den Emmausjüngern und den Aposteln: Das Lateinische Peregrinispiel," *Germanistische Abhandlungen*, LXII (1930), 56-61.

This meant that no matter how far a man should venture forth on the surface of the earth he was everywhere equally a stranger, equally detached from the things of this world and always equidistant from God. Whereas for most people this remained a theoretical concept, the missionary could give it a concrete form by purposely selecting the life of a stranger, and travel into the unknown regions. The fear for mythical monsters and a thousand other perils which detained the ordinary man were immaterial to him, for the worst that could happen to him was death and to die in the service of his faith was for a true missionary cause for elation rather than concern. Friar Bieul takes into account the possibility of death; he only hopes that Christ will give him enough strength to endure it:

> Affin aussi que le précieux sanc Jhésu Crist espandus pour nostre sauvement me feust confort et donnast vigueur et enforcement de sa foy prechier et se cas si offrist mourir pour celui que moy donna la vie. [15]

> Also [I hoped] that the precious blood which Jesus Christ shed for our salvation would give me comfort, vigor and strength to preach His faith and, if necessary, to die for Him who gave me life.

The missionary, then, travelling for a spiritual purpose, possesses a powerful consolation that fortifies him for any adverse event. Thus paradoxically, while medieval Christian thought downgraded the intrinsic value of travelling, it provided a strong impetus for it by putting it at the service of the faith. Without this backing which his faith afforded the apostolic traveller, the discovery of unknown lands would have lacked a decisive motivating force and would very likely have been far more difficult to achieve.

The accounts of discoverers and chroniclers of later ages bear out this assumption. Both Vasco da Gama and Columbus were impelled in large part by a sense of Christian mission, the extent of which has already been cited. The exultation of Columbus at finding a large pagan population to be converted was especially great. The enthusiasm of his admirers matched his own and his

---

[15] *Relation du voyage du frère Bieul,* p. 258.

discovery was glorified *ex post facto* as an indication of Divine mission. The proof was seen in his name which in its latinized form means "Christ-bearer." Of this contemporary belief the analysis of Bartolomé de las Casas is characteristic:

> Llamóse, pues, por nombre, Cristóbal, conviene a saber, *Cristum ferens*, quiere decir traedor o llevador de Cristo, y así se afirmaba él algunas veces; como en la verdad él haya sido el primero que abrió las puertas deste mar Oceano por donde entró y él metió a estas tierras tan remotas y reinos hasta entonces tan incógnitas a Nuestro Salvador Jesucristo y a su bendito nombre. [16]

> His name was Cristóbal, that is to say, *Christum ferens*, which means "bringer or bearer of Christ," and he himself confirmed this several times; since indeed he was the first to open the gates of this ocean, through which he entered and introduced our Saviour Jesus Christ and His blessed name into those distant lands and hitherto unknown kingdoms.

Whereas Columbus was not only a missionary but also a secular envoy sent to seek trade with the Orient, the calling of Saint Francis Xavier (1506-1552) was entirely apostolic. He travelled the Orient widely and was one of the few westerners allowed to enter xenophobic Japan. In a letter to Ignacio de Loyola he, like his medieval predecessors, characterizes his voyage as a *peregrinatio:*

> De la ciudad de Goa os escreví muy largo de toda nuestra pelegrinación despues que partimos de Lisboa asta nuestra llegada en la Yndia.... [17]

> From the city of Goa I wrote you quite extensively about our journey from our departure from Lisbon to our arrival in India....

---

[16] See *Historia de las Indias, BAE*, XCV, 21b. On a map drawn by Columbus's cartographer Juan de la Cosa, Columbus is iconographically represented as Christophorus with the Christ child on his shoulders wading through water. See map in A. Rein, *Die Europäische Ausbreitung über die Erde* (Potsdam, 1931), p. 84.

[17] Letter to Ignacio de Loyola, in *Epistolae S. Francisci aliqui eius scripta,* eds. G. Schurhammer, J. Wicki (Rome, 1944), I, 146-147.

The remainder of his letter testifies that his journey is guided by an ulterior motive, namely the extension of the influence of Christianity:

> En estos lugares, quando [yo] llegava, bautizava todos los monachos que no eran bautizados. [18]

> When I arrived in those places I baptized all the monks which had not yet been baptized.

PEREGRINATIO and the Christian Search for the Earthly Paradise

Yet, while the Renaissance seafarer found in the missionary ideal ample justification for reconnoitering unknown regions, and while a medieval Christian doctrine provided consolation for the fearful moments of his journey, he lacked the precedents of the sea voyages themselves. There had of course been the voyages of the Vikings which took place throughout the Middle Ages. But these were accomplished by a people only recently christianized, who continued to sack the coastlines of Europe with pagan vigor long after the remaining Germanic tribes had acquiesced in the Christian yoke. Their transatlantic exploits to Iceland, Greenland, and perhaps also to America, magnificent as they were, received only marginal attention. Since they were not undertaken for any specifically Christian purpose — the only one which Medieval Europe would recognize [19] — their achievements would not elicit the attention the deserved.

Instead Europeans delighted in reading accounts of mythical voyages. Some of these had a factual origin, though far less spectacular than the Norsemen's, but their Christian purpose arounsed widespread attention, and much imagination was lavished to embellish them far beyond their original scope. One of the most popular of these tales was that of St. Brendan, the sixth-century Irish monk, whose adventures survive in eighty manuscripts still extant. [20] They describe his journey westward into the Atlantic

---

[18] *Epistolae*, I, 147.

[19] See our not 9 on page 28.

[20] E. G. R. Waters, ed., *The Anglo-Norman Voyage of St. Brendan by Benedeit* (Oxford, 1928), p. lxxxii.

Ocean in search of the earthly Paradise, the *terra repromissionis sanctorum,* which he and his companions finally reach after seven years of endless navigation. On his way he stops on various wondrous islands inhabited by hermits, meets frightening monsters, and sees the mouth of Hell where Judas is tormented. After a brief stop at Paradise he returns with precious gems to testify to his presence there.

Although St. Brendan's voyage depicted a strictly Christian aim with its search for Paradise, the writer's delight with the marvels encountered is apparent, as it is in the earliest available and most popular of the accounts, the eleventh-century *Navigatio Sancti Brendani.* Its noteworthy feature is that it begins with a comprehensive description of Paradise before St. Brendan actually sets out on his voyage. Brendan as well as the reader is consequently deprived of the suspense surrounding the actual discovery of Paradise, with the result that the interest shifts from the destination of the voyage itself to the marvelous things encountered in its course. This feature is stylistically characterized by the persistent recurrence of the temporal *cum* which signals the irruption of new and surprising events, "While they were travelling along, there appeared to them ...," as in the following examples:

> Cum autem nauigassent iuxta insulam ubi erant per triduum antea ... viderunt aliam insulam.... [21]

> When they sailed close to the island where they had been three days before ... they saw another island....

> Cum autem appropinquassent ad locum ubi ascendere debuissent de naui, ecce apparuit illis cacabus.... [22]

> And when they reached the place where they were to climb out of their ship, behold, a cacabus[-bird] appeared before them....

---

[21] *Navigatio Sancti Brendani abbatis,* ed. Carl Selmer, *Publications in Medieval Studies* (Notre Dame, Indiana, 1959), p. 22.

[22] *Navigatio,* p. 42.

In each case the emphasis is on a strong sense of discovery and surprise — *ecce!* The objects appear in the path of St. Brendan as if someone deliberately placed them there to acquaint him with as many novelties as possible. Later he finds that it is in fact the hand of God that provided him with the discoveries, a fact that is disclosed to him when he reaches Paradise:

> Ecce terram quam quesisti per multum tempus. Ideo non potuisti statim illam invenire quia Deus uoluit tibi ostendere diversa sua secreta in oceano magno. [23]

> Behold the land for which you have searched a long time! The reason that you were not able to find it sooner is that God intended to display to you His manifold mysteries on the great ocean.

God, then, deliberately stalled the progress of his journey to give him ample opportunity for discovery, to introduce him to the secrets of the vast, unknown ocean. It is for this reason, too, that the voyage takes seven years on its way to Paradise, whereas the return takes far less time.

It is noteworthy that in a twelfth-century Anglo-Norman version of the *Navigatio* the above-quoted sentence is missing in the re-rendering, a fact which its editor, E. G. R. Waters, attributes to a difference of focus in the motivation of each version. He observes that, whereas the *Navigatio* indulges the curiosity of the travellers by its emphasis on the things to be seen, the Anglo-Norman author adds passages that enhance the ascetic nature of the journey. [24] When the monks are frightened by a sea monster, St. Brendan reminds them that God's intention is to instruct them by these sights, so that they may become even more fervent believers:

> Ne merveillés de ço, seignurs.
> Pur ço vus volt Deus ci mener
> Que il vus voleit plus asener.

---

[23] *Navigatio*, p. 80. A later version of the *Navigatio* alters the title to *Peregrinatio*. See *Peregrinatio Sancti Brendani*, ed. C. Schröder (Erlangen, 1871).

[24] Waters, ed., p. ciii.

Ses merveilles cum plus verrez,
En lui mult mielz puis encrerrez. [25]

Be not startled at this, gentlemen. God wanted you to stop here so He could show you more. The more of His miracles you see the more firmly you will believe.

The longer the voyage the greater are the hardships to be endured:

Grant curs unt fait il pelerin,
Mais uncore ne sevent fin;
E nepurtant ne s'en feignent,
Mais cum plus vunt, plus se peinent,
Ne de peiner se recrerrunt
De ci que lur desir verrunt. (11. 1101-1106)

The pilgrims have gone a long way, and still they perceive no end to it. Nevertheless they are not discouraged; rather the further they go the more they endure. Nor do the hardships cause them to lose faith so long as they see the goal of their desire.

There is no end in sight for their toils; nevertheless the voyagers refuse to be diverted by them, because in their calling as *pelerin* they have renounced the comforts of the world. They are convinced that the discipline and the mortification inflicted on their bodies will ingratiate them in the eyes of God:

Sainz hoem cum ad plusurs travailz—
De faim, de seif, de freiz, de calz,
Ainxe, tristur e granz poürs—
De tant vers Deu creist sis oürs.
Eisi est d'els, puis q'unt voüd
U li dampnét sunt reçoüd.
En Deu ferment lur fiance,
N'i aturnent mescreance.
Vunt s'en avant, ne dutent rien,
Quar ço sevent que espleitent bien. (11. 1177-1186)

The more hardships a holy man experiences—such as hunger, thirst, cold, heart, worry, sadness and great fear— the more his good fortune grows in the eyes of God.

---

[25] *Anglo-Norman Voyage*, ll. 471-476.

Such is their lot after they have seen [the place] where the damned are housed. They affirm their faith in God, and do not turn to disbelief. They proceed without misgivings, for they know that they will be well rewarded.

They are assured of their future rewards, "sevent que espleitent bien," though it remains ambiguous whether they will consist in the finding of the terrestrial Paradise or of the Heavenly one after death. The word *pelerin* accommodates both interpretations. On the one hand, they are like the *pelerin*, the hermit St. Ailbe, who by his self-inflicted exile hopes to gain the Heavenly Paradise. [26] On the other hand, their voyage to the earthly one is also called a *peregrinatio,* as when a bird foretells St. Brendan the duration of his voyage:

Deus proposuit uobis quattuor loca per quattuor tempora usque dum finiantur septem anni peregrinacionis uestre. [27]

God will put before you four places for four seasons, until the seven years of your pilgrimage are completed.

An old Italian version of around 1300 expresses the goal of their voyage with even more precision:

Dipo' i .vii. anni del vosso pelegrinaggio troverrete Terra di Ripromessione di Sancti, quella che voi dimandate, et quine strete .xl. dì, poi vi recra Dio ala terra dela nativita vossa. [28]

After the seventh year of your pilgrimage you will find the Promised Land of the saints that you sought. And you will remain there for forty days, after which God will return you to the land of your birth.

The search for Paradise then is inextricably bound up with the exercise of an ascetic life, as we observe it also in such similar quests as the *Iter ad paradisum* where Alexander must cross dif-

---

[26] *Anglo-Norman Voyage,* line 722.

[27] *Navigatio,* p. 43.

[28] *An Old Italian Version of the Navigatio Sancti Brendani,* ed. E. G. R. Waters, in *Publications of the Philological Society,* X (Oxford, 1931), 61.

ficult terrain for days before he reaches it. [29] Or it may not be reachable at all as in the case of Macarios who spends a lifetime in the vicinity of Paradise, but is forbidden by an angel to enter it. [30] The sufferings and privations which the searcher undergoes are at the same time a purgation and edification of the soul, so that the geographical *peregrinatio* is accompanied by a spiritual one.

This dual *peregrinatio* also pertains to other medieval visions that purport a location of Paradise within a concrete geographical sphere. In the *Tractatus de Purgatorio Sancti Patricii* (1150), for example, the entrance to Purgatory is thought to be located in Hibernia (Ireland). The author, Henricus Salteriensis, does not, however, commit himself to a definite judgment on its location, preferring instead to accept the words of others on faith:

> Idcirco, quae de loco ipsius purgatorii, de tempore pur-
> gationis, de modo purgandi se, sive conficiendi ipsam
> peregrinationem ... ex relatu aliorum accepi; sed talium
> de quorum fide mihi dubitandum non fuit. [31]

> As for the location of this Purgatory, the time and manner
> of purgation and the accomplishment of this pilgrimage,
> I learned that from the reports of others. But [I chose
> only] those whose fidelity I had no cause to doubt.

The knight Oenus who undertakes the *peregrinatio* therefore moves within a geographic location, but at the same time his undertaking has the purpose of purging him of the sins incurred in his dissipated life.

Henricus' uncertainty is not surprising, for the issue of the location was considerably disputed in his time. In the first place, the idea of the original Eden persisting somewhere in concrete form was problematic in the eyes of St. Augustine, who stressed the allegorical conception of it. [32] Nevertheless the debate

---

[29] J. K. Wright, *The Geographical Lore of the Time of the Crusades* (New York, 1965), pp. 262-263.

[30] Wright, p. 262.

[31] Henricus Salteriensis, *Tractatus de Purgatorio Sancti Patricii*, PL, CLXXX, 977.

[32] Wright, p. 262.

continued undeterred. Whereas St. Brendan's *Navigatio* places it in the west, the majority of texts such as the *Romance of Alexander* and Peter Lombard's *Sententiae* place it in the east.[33] So strong was the conviction of its existence that it appeared on the *mappaemundi,* the medieval maps of the known world.[34] Some medieval travelers who professed to have traversed Asia also felt obliged to enter on a discussion of Paradise. Thus John Maundeville, for example, admits that his only information is based on hearsay: "Of Paradise ne can I speken propurly; for I was not there. It is fer bezonde; and that forthinkethe me: and also I was not worthy."[35] Thus, far from disbelieving its existence, he blames his inability to reach it on his own moral shortcomings.

One of the most prominent treatments of the issue was Dante's *Divina Commedia.* Whereas almost everybody else was uncertain about the location of Paradise, he was not. With the love of symmetry and logical cohesion so dear to the scholastic mind, he sets forth the location of Purgatory and Paradise with geometric accuracy. Whereas St. Patrick's Purgatory is below ground, Dante places it above in the form of a mountain in order to contrast it to the location of Hell below ground, and to symbolize the process of moral ascension that accompanies purgation. The mountain is located in the unknown regions of the southern hemisphere, the "antipodes," and it bears on its summit the earthly Paradise.

Yet the geometric perfection of his universe is deceptive since it is not based on empirical geographic knowledge but on a mixture of Ptolemaic theory, Christian myth, and speculative scholasticism. It is a "Christian topography" in which the shape and concept of the universe is determined by dogmatic truth rather than geographic knowledge, and whose dimensions are spiritual rather than physical.[36] Correspondingly the journey is

---

[33] Wright, pp. 261-263. For a discussion of the medieval preoccupation with Paradise, see also Howard R. Patch, *The Other World According to Descriptions in Medieval Literature* (Cambridge, Mass., 1950).

[34] Wright, p. 262.

[35] *The Voiage and Travaile of Sir John Maundeville,* ed. J. O. Halliwell (London, 1883), p. 303. This is an edition of the 1563 translation from the original French.

[36] χριστιανικὴ τοπογραφία is the title of a geographical treatise of the sixth-century traveler Cosmas Indicopleustes. See *The Christian Topography,*

meant to represent a spiritual displacement rather than a physical one: It has its beginning "nel mezzo del cammin di nostra vita," in the path of our life, where the plural *nostra* signifies that part of life which Dante has in common with his readers, namely the spiritual life of every Christian. His path, then, can be said to be located on a spiritual landscape. Having lost himself in a "selva selvaggia," the jungle of his soul's disorder, it is the spirit of his revered model Vergil who offers him assistance in escaping his dilemma.

Vergil leads him onto another path, through Hell and through Purgatory. Upon arrival on the island of Purgatory, other souls ask them for the way to the mountain. Vergil is unable to help them and replies:

> Voi credete
> forse che siamo esperti d'este loco
> ma noi siam peregrin come voi siete. [37]

> Perhaps you think that we are acquainted with this place, but we are strangers [here] just like you.

He signifies that he and Dante are *peregrini*, strangers to whom the spiritual countryside of Purgatory is unfamiliar. But with respect to Dante the word *peregrini* also bears the overtone of the penitential condition that he has in common with the other souls. For whereas in Hell he was merely a spectator, he is also a participant in Purgatory. His journey thus becomes a purgative *peregrinatio* similar to that of Oenus in the Purgatory of St. Patrick. For Dante as for Oenus the purgation is a necessary precondition for the attainment of Paradise and in his case also of Beatrice, a fact of which Vergil reminds him when he hesitates to traverse the purifying wall of fire:

---

ed. E. O. Winstedt (Cambridge, 1909). Cosmas' concept about the shape of the universe exemplifies an extreme dependence on Biblical exegesis. He rejected the idea of a spherical world in favor of a box-like shape that resembled the Lord's Tabernacle.

[37] Dante Alighieri, *Purgatorio*, ed. John D. Sinclair (New York, 1961), Canto II, ll. 61-63.

Or vedi, figlio,
tra Beatrice e te è questo muro. [38]

Look my son, between Beatrice and you is [only] this
wall.

This and other elements of penitence are the toll that must be
paid. Without it one may not pass on to the desired goal, and it
is exacted of everyone without exception. Dante with his special
status as a visitor would have preferred to avoid it since his mission is primarily exploratory, the reconnaissance of the *ultra mun-
dum*. But the addition of the penitence broadens the scope of
his mission into an act of self-improvement, an *itinerarium mentis
in Deum*. [39]

The Search for Paradise and Geographical Discovery

The quests for Paradise continued long after Dante as an issue
for literary minds as well as for explorers themselves, as illustrated
by Columbus, who earnestly suspects Paradise of being somewhere
in the area of the Orinoco River and enthusiastically dispatches
his brother Bartolomé on the search. [40] Even as late as 1666 there
appears in London *A Discourse of the Terrestrial Paradise*, which
contains a serious and laborious inquiry into the question of the
location of the Garden of Eden. Though the author foregoes any
definite conclusion, he is confident that his book will serve as the
hitherto best source for further research by others. [41]

On the other hand the English poet Michael Drayton (1563-
1631) is less uncertain, and when he decides on Virginia as the
site for Paradise he merely recalls that it was one of the possible

---

[38] *Purgatorio*, XXVII, ll. 35-36.

[39] The *Itinerarium mentis in Deum* is an ascetic treatise by St. Bonaventure. The term has been applied to the *Commedia* by Charles Singleton,
Dante Studies (Cambridge, Mass., 1958), II, 4.

[40] *Cartas de relación de la conquista de América*, I, 55.

[41] *A Discourse of the Terrestrial Paradise, aiming at a more probable
discovery of the true situation of that happy place of our first parents
habitation*, printed by James Fletcher (London, 1666), p. 166.

locations considered in his time. In a poem exhorting the interest of colonizers for Virginia, he advertises it in this manner:

> Virginia,
> Earth's only Paradise;
> ... ...
> To whom the Golden Age
> Still Nature's laws doth give. [42]

It is interesting that Drayton connects Paradise with the Golden Age, alluding to the fusion of the Christian and pagan myths that is becoming increasingly characteristic in his time. Already St. Boniface describes Paradise as *amoenitatis locus*, a term which E. R. Curtius has established as a topos of pagan extraction. [43] In the Anglo-Norman play of Adam, the stage setting similarly calls for decorations to conform with the concept. [44] In Spenser's *Shepheard's Calender* (1579) this is expressed even more specifically, as the shepherd Collins equates his Arcadian idyll with Paradise:

> O happie Hobbinoll, I blesse thy state,
> That Paradise hast found which Adam lost. [45]

PEREGRINATIO: *The Voyage of Discovery in Literature*

With such increasing identification of the Christian and the pagan paradise, the question arises as to what extent a quest for the former would correspond to the latter. In *Canto IX* of *Os Lusíadas*, the voyagers encounter on their return trip from India an island with an Arcadian setting. It is the "ilha de Venus," populated with beautiful sea-nymphs and endowed with all the

---

[42] R. Shafer, "Virginia," *From Beowulf to Thomas Hardy* (New York, 1939), I, 512.

[43] E. R. Curtius, *European Literature and the Latin Middle Ages* (New York, 1963), p. 200.

[44] Curtius, p. 200.

[45] Edmund Spenser, *Shepheard's Calender,* June, in *The Works of Edmund Spenser,* ed. John Todd (London, 1877), p. 378. Spenser's gloss reads "A Paradise in Greeke, signifieth a garden of pleasure, or place of delights" (p. 379).

attributes of the *locus amoenus*. It is therefore thoroughly pagan, especially since the goddess is known to possess not one but many such islands, quite in contrast to the Christian claim that there is only one.

Venus prepares the island for the seafarers as "premio, e doce gloria / Do trabalho," that is, as a reward for the hardships which the "mísera gente peregrina" have experienced. A comparison with St. Brendan's quest is in order here, for there too the glimpse of the *terra repromissionis sanctorum* is a reward for the toils of the *peregrini*. Yet the monks pursue their goal for its own sake and direct all their efforts toward attaining it, whereas for Vasco da Gama the "ilha de Venus" is only an incidental discovery on the road to the primary objective, the finding of a path to India. It is present in the poem not to obey a spiritual demand but to fulfill an esthetic criterion. [46] Camões wishes to give epic proportions to an historical event to let the deeds of da Gama rival the fame of the ancients:

> Cessem do sábio Grego e do Troiano
> As navegações grandes que fizeram;
> ... ...
> Que eu canto o peito illustre lusitano,
> A quem Neptuno e Marte obedeceram! [47]

> Let us cease [mentioning] the long journeys which the astute Greek [Ulysses] and the Trojan [Aeneas] accomplished.... For I shall sing of the splendid Lusitanian courage, to which both Neptune and Mars paid homage.

To achieve the epic effect he does not merely narrate, but in the true tradition he "sings":

---

[46] Perhaps because of this the paganized paradise of the Renaissance epic could not readily join into a natural spiritual unity with the poem as did the Christian Paradise in medieval works. It remained an unmanageable adjunct which aggravated the epic's problem of integration, as A. Bartlett Giamatti observes in *The Earthly Paradise and the Renaissance Epic* (Princeton, 1966). In general, he feels that due to the clash between pagan and Christian mythologies "the successful Christian epic proved an impossible task" (p. 224).

[47] *Os Lusíadas*, I, 3.

As armas e os barões assinalados

... ...

Cantando espalharei por toda parte. [48]

[The fame of] the arms and the distinguished men I shall spread everywhere [with my] singing.

He also exploits myths that captivate his contemporaries by their esthetic appeal. The toilsome *peregrinatio* for a utopian paradise was evidently an appealing topic, a fact that is also borne out by the work of Camões' near-contemporary Torquato Tasso, *La Gerusalemme liberata* (1580).

In *Canto XV* of *La Gerusalemme* two knights search for the famed Christian knight Rinaldo, who had been thought dead but who had been pronounced alive by a soothsayer. Taking leave from Godfrey of Bouillon's crusader army in the Holy Land, they set out across the Mediterranean, pass the Pillars of Hercules,

---

[48] *Os Lusíadas,* I, 1-2. One recalls the opening lines of the *Aeneid,* "Arma virumque cano. ..." Cf. also *Orlando Furioso,* I, 1: "Le donne, i cavallier, l'arme, gli amori, ... io canto." Also in *La Gerusalemme liberata,* I, 1: "Canto l'arme pietose. ..." Appropriately perhaps, the fourteenth-century predecessors of Ariosto were known as *cantastorie.* That is, through the act of singing the poet personalized the otherwise anonymous epic material of the *storia,* thereby claiming dominion over it. His successor, the courtly epic writer of the Renaissance, no longer actually "sang." But the previously established posture of the personalizing "singer" intervening in his narrative remained a tradition. For the poet it was a convenient posture, because it allowed him to demonstrate, like a *Deus artifex,* his creative dominion over the narrative. (See Robert M. Durling, *The Figure of the Poet in Renaissance Epic* [Cambridge, Mass., 1965], esp. Ch. V.) This practice also appears prominently in Ercilla's *Araucana.* See Juan B. Avalle-Arce, "El poeta en su poema," *Revista de Occidente,* XCV (1971), 152-170.

Once the poet's intervention became accepted as a tradition, the nature of his intervention could vary. Not only could it have an artistic purpose but a spiritual one as well. For example, in the following divinized version of the *topos,* written in 1584, Fray Gabriel de la Mata intervenes not to parade his creative bravura, but to emphasize his personal devotion to St. Francis:

> Las armas canto que a un varón sagrado
> Hicieron invencible en este suelo. ...

I sing of the arms which made a brave holy man invincible here on earth. ...

Cited from Bruce W. Wardropper, *Historia de la poesía lírica a lo divino* (Madrid, 1958), p. 49.

and finally reach the *isole felici* (Canary Islands). On one of the islands they find Rinaldo as a happy prisoner of the Queen of the Nymphs, Armida, and they succeed in persuading him to rejoin the crusaders.

Upon reaching the pleasant isle they are greeted by nymphs who invite them to stay and make love to them,

> Oh fortunati *peregrin,* cui lice
> giungere in questa sede alma e felice! [49]

> Oh happy wanderers who are privileged to reach this blessed and happy location!

But the seafarers refuse because their primary mission is not to seek enjoyment but to recover Rinaldo. As with Vasco da Gama, their finding of the *locus amoenus* is an accidental experience. Tasso, however, exploits it eagerly as a part of the theme of discovery that occupies his contemporaries. Thus for example when the knights pass the Pillars of Hercules they are informed of how Ulysses braved the interdict *nec plus ultra* and perished. [50] When they show their eagerness to explore the *isole felici,* they are told that the time for their discovery has not come yet, and that to act contrariwise would be to oppose God's will:

> ché ancor volto non è lo spacio intero
> ch'al grande scoprimento ha fisso Dio;
> né lece a voi da l'ocean profundo
> recar vera notizia al vostro mondo. (XV, 39)

> The period [of time] for which God has destined the discoveries has not yet been completed. You are not allowed to report any precise information about the great ocean to your people.

Future men, above all Columbus, are destined to discover the unknown lands.

The length of the episode — more than two cantos — testifies that Tasso was assured of the interest of the readers in the theme

---

[49] Torquato Tasso, *La Gerusalemme liberata,* ed. Giovanni Getto (Brescia, 1960), Canto XV, v. 62.

[50] *La Gerusalemme,* XV, 26.

and that he apparently did not fear its excessive diversion from the affairs of the Holy War. Indeed the voyagers never forget their mission of finding Rinaldo which means the enhancing of the cause of the crusaders. They do not stop to follow up their discoveries or to enjoy the delights of the *locus amoenus*. They are at all times conscious of the calling, and of the fact that they are part of the crusading host, the *arme peregrine*. [51] Thus when they are greeted as *peregrini* by the nymphs, they are defined by their dual role as crusaders and as discoverers. It was customary furthermore to term the crusades as voyages going *ultra mare*, as in *La gran conquista de ultramar*. Their sea voyages, on the other hand, are more literally directed *ultra mare*, "overseas." The *peregrinatio* of their voyage, then, is nominally related to the *peregrinatio* of the crusade, in that it becomes a subordinate episode within the larger scope of action which the affairs of the Holy War represent.

In the *Soledades* (1613) of Góngora the meaning of "discovery, travel" is likewise included in the more inclusive meaning-cluster of *peregrinatio*. The plot of the poem describes the fate of a shipwrecked youth, known only as *el peregrino*. He arrives in a bucolic world and his early contacts with its inhabitants reveal them to be people of the simple virtues reminiscent of the Golden Age from which they are not far removed. This condition of the integral rural life of the pastoral community closely resembles the commonplace idyllic visions of the sixteenth and seventeenth century that embody an escape from reality.

Góngora enhances the unreality of his vision by his stylistic perfection of the *cultista* traits. The metaphorical abstraction and transformation of reality, the inversion of syntax, the use of uncommon vocabulary, reveal a desire to idealize, to remove poetic expression as far as possible from the common, the well-known expression, to escape to new esthetic norms in another realm. It

---

[51] *La Gerusalemme*, I, 77; also IX, 4. In medieval chronicles crusades were often called *peregrinationes*. See e.g., *Das Itinerarium peregrinorum* in *Schriften der Monumenta Germaniae Historia*, ed. H. E. Mayer (Stuttgart, 1962), XVIII. *Peregrinatio* thus signifies "warfare in the service of Christianity" and represents a special application of the *militia Christi*. See our Chapter III.

is in a sense a flight into an esthetic no-man's-land. To create poetry which will embody this escape is a difficult undertaking, as Góngora attests:

> Pasos de un peregrino son errante
> cuantos me dictó versos dulce musa:
> en soledad confusa
> perdidos unos, otros inspirados. [52]

All these verses, which the sweet muse dictated to me, are the steps of an errant wanderer; in the confused solitude some [are] lost, others inspired.

The verses are "pasos de un peregrino errante," i.e., they are constantly in danger of going astray in "soledad confusa." If the verses are the "pasos," the steps, then the "peregrino" is the poet himself who undertakes the risky journey to the desired goal, the poetic utopia. By calling himself "peregrino" he acknowledges his kinship with his brainchild, the *peregrino* within the poem. While the latter moves within an idealized pastoral world, the former too passes through an ideal poetic world which Dámaso Alonso calls a "mundo abreviado, renovado y puro." [53] The condition of the lonely traveler in a wonderland in this way reflects the poet's own status. He realizes that the practice of his brand of poetry is a lonely pursuit, to be mastered only by a select elite who possess the proper inspiration. Its appreciation is likewise reserved for the few. Just as Dante recognized that his *Paradiso* was "pan delli angeli," [54] to be appreciated only by the true

---

[52] Luis de Góngora, *Las soledades,* ed. Dámaso Alonso (Madrid, 1956), ll. 1-4.

[53] See Alonso's introduction to *Las soledades,* p. 32.

[54] Dante, *Paradiso,* II, 11. Dante also employs the metaphor of the voyage into the unknown to illustrate the extraordinary nature of his poetic undertaking. Thus he urges those who are unable to follow him to stay behind:

> O voi che siete in piccioletta barca,
> desiderosi d'ascoltar, seguiti
> dietro al mio legno che cantando varca,
> tornate a riveder li vostri liti:
> non vi mettete in pelago, chè, forse,
> perdendo me, rimarreste smarriti.
> L'acqua ch'io prendo già mai non si corse.

(*Paradiso,* II, 1-7)

connoisseur, Góngora's poetry, too, was destined for the initiate, as the controversies among his contemporaries indicate.

Another exploitation of the seafaring *peregrinatio* is exemplified by Rabelais' *Pantagruel* (1532). In Book IV Pantagruel sets out in quest of the oracle of the Bacbuc, the bottle whose enclosed wisdom shall help him decide whether or not he should marry. After a westward journey to China which includes numerous stops at fabulous islands, he finds the bottle whose comic-enigmatic advice is *Trink*. Even without this comic anti-climax it is evident that the purpose of Pantagruel's voyage is less important than the imaginative exploitation of the motif itself. We never find out, for example, whether or not Pantagruel will ever marry, even though this problem occupied him throughout the greater part of Book III. Instead the account focuses on the things found in the course of the voyage. The mention of the Northwest Passage to China alone was an issue of sufficient interest to the contemporary reading public. Rabelais capitalizes on it by strewing the path of the expedition with fantastic islands populated by chitterlings and deformed human beings living in strange relationships. His aim is to confront Pantagruel with a maximum of surprising incidents and to elicit thereby his infinite curiosity. It is, in fact, his primary aim as evidenced by the conversation between Panurge and Pantagruel in which they decide on the voyage:

> [Panurge:] Je vous seray un Achates, un Damis, et compaignon en tout le voyage. Je vous ay long temps cogneu amateur de pérégrinité, et desyrant tous jours veoir et tous jours apprendre. Nous verrons chose admirables, et m'en croyez.
>
> Volontiers, respondit Pantagruel. Mais, avant nous mettre en ceste longue pérégrination, plène de azard, plène de dangiers evidens. ... [55]

Oh you, in a little bark, [who are] eager to listen, who have followed my craft, which makes its way singing.

Turn back to see your shore again! Do not venture onto the ocean, for perhaps you will lose me and go astray.

The waters on which I embark have never been sailed before.

[55] *Œuvres complètes de Rabelais,* ed. Jean Plattard (Paris, 1929), III, Chapter 47.

> [Panurge:] I will be an Achates to you, a Damon, and
> a companion for the whole journey. I have long known
> you to be a lover of travelling, one who always wishes to
> see and learn. We shall see marvelous things, believe me.
> "I am quite willing," Pantagruel replied, "but before we
> embark on this long journey, so full of risks, so full of
> manifest dangers. . . .

Panurge characterizes his pupil as an *amateur de pérégrinité*, a
"lover of travel," who desires forever to see and to learn. Significantly he uses the abstract noun *pérégrinité* to indicate the
condition, i.e., the status rather than the act, of wandering and
being on the move. For Pantagruel then the particular *peregrinatio*
to China is only a part of his condition as a wandering observer,
whose life is dedicated to the satisfaction of his curiosity, to the
endless learning that characterizes the spirit of Humanism. Quite
fittingly he belongs to a race of giants, so that in him all the
human characteristics are exaggerated beyond proportion: he is
among other things a monster of curiosity. And as his desire to
discover the world is boundless, so is the variety of objects which
the author provides for him. For the content of the subject matter
as well as the style of the narration exceeds all imaginable norms.
The monstrous exploits of Gargantua and Pantagruel, the perpetual recourse to obscenity, the endless exploitation of trivia that
serve to elicit his wit, the spurious word-formations, all of these
elements contribute to the construction of an expanding hybrid
universe in which the existence of everything that man can imagine
is tolerated.

The exact nature of Pantagruel's learning process is illuminated
when one compares his *peregrinatio* to that of Andrenio in *El
criticón*, written by Baltasar Gracián over a century later, in 1651.
Andrenio, who is called a *peregrino,* is a talented but unlearned
savage touring the world in the company of his tutor Critilo in
order to get to know it better. Just as Pantagruel begins his voyage
with his characteristic exuberance for the things of this world, so
Andrenio, too, begins his own with a vision of the plenitude of the
world that had been imparted to him in a dream. [56] Yet Panta-

---

[56] Baltasar Gracián, *El criticón, ed. M. Romera-Navarro* (London, Philadelphia, 1938), Part I, Chapter 2.

gruel's education consists merely in the apprehension of an infinite number of objects, whereas his attitude towards them remains the same. Andrenio's outlook, on the other hand, is decisively changed. He learns that the world which he thought to be a beautiful and harmonious construct, an unblemished *mundo,* as indeed it was originally, had been spoiled by man and had become *inmundo,* tarnished. His tutor, moreover, does not allow him to view events and objects for their own sake, but abstracts them into object lessons. He teaches his pupil to be critical, to distinguish between virtue and vice, to guard himself against evil through superior discernment. To acquire these skills is to become proficient in *prudencia.* Andrenio's *peregrinatio,* then, is a peripatetic apprenticeship in *prudencia.* "Step by step" his geographical displacement is accompanied by a spiritual displacement of a gradual *desengaño,* the change of attitude that is at the heart of the Christian *peregrinatio.*

The distance which separates Pantagruel and Andrenio thus illustrates the difference between the non-Christian and the Christian exploitation of the voyage theme. We find a further example of this development in the literary treatments of the wanderings of Ulysses. Tasso describes him as a *peregrino:*

> Giaceva esposto il peregrino Ulisse
> Mesto ed ignudo sovra i lidi asicutti. [57]

> Sad and naked the wanderer Ulysses lay exposed on the dry shore.

Ever since Dante the notion that Ulysses passed and perished beyond the Pillars of Hercules was a popular one, [58] which Tasso too touches upon in *La Gerusalemme liberata* (1580). [59] The Spaniard Juan de Arguijo also names him a *peregrino:*

> Con heroica grandeza el sabio griego
> cantó de aquel astuto Peregrino

---

[57] Torquato Tasso, "Rime," in *Opere,* ed. Bruno Maier (Milano, 1963), I, 669.

[58] *Inferno,* XXVI. See also W. B. Stanford, *The Ulysses Theme* (Oxford, 1963), Chapter 14.

[59] Tasso, *La Gerusalemme,* XV, 26.

> el luengo discurrir, cuyo camino
> tuvo por fin de Itaca el sosiego. [60]

With heroic greatness the wise Greek [Homer] sang of the long erring of that astute wanderer whose trail at last came to a rest in Ithaca.

A dramatic elaboration of the motif also appears in Calderón de la Barca's drama *El mayor encanto amor* (1639), that presents Ulysses' love affair with Circe. Ulysses arrives at the shores of her island as *peregrino* and *náufrago,* and the love-starved Circe, overjoyed at his arrival, proceeds to lull him into amorous oblivion with all the charms at her disposal. The environment is conducive to her purpose as it possesses all the attributes of the *locus amoenus:*

> Hospedaje de Saturno
>
> . . . .
>
> Selva sí de Amor y Venus
> Deleitoso paraíso. [61]

A hospice of Saturn ... a delightful paradise of Love and Venus.

With time, however, he regains the proper consciousness of his goal, realizing that the return to Ithaca is the real destiny of his *peregrinatio,* and that this haphazard encounter with the paradise of love only distracts him dangerously from this destiny. He therefore flees the island, happy that reason has saved him from the powerful charms of Circe.

The conflict of reason and inclination is decisively stressed in Calderón's allegorized version of the play, the *auto sacramental* entitled *Los encantos de la culpa* (1649). Here the "cristiano Ulises" represents El Hombre, Everyman:

> El hombre soy, a astucias inclinado,
> y por serlo hoy Ulises me he nombrado,
> que en griego decir quiere

---

[60] Laudatory sonnet in Lope de Vega's *Peregrino en su patria,* in *Colección de las obras sueltas* (Madrid, 1777), V, viii.

[61] *El mayor encanto amor,* BAE, VII, 394c.

cauteloso, y así, quien ya quisiere
corra las líneas de la suerte mía;
de Ulises siga en mí la alegoría,
y los que en una parte
me llamaron viador, viendo mi arte,
y en otra navegante, que el camino
del mar discurro siempre peregrino. [62]

I am Man, inclined to cunning, and because of that I
have now taken the name of Ulysses which in Greek
means "crafty." Now, then, whoever might wish to pursue
the trail of my fortune may follow the allegory of Ulysses
in me. [That includes those of you] who on occasion
called me a traveller on observing my skill, and those
who called me a navigator, seeing that I cross the sea
always like a wanderer.

The island, named *jardín ameno* and *paraíso*, is inhabited by La
Culpa, the sin and guilt that is embodied by Circe. El Hombre
characterizes her as

horror de aquestos desiertos
y Circe de estas montañas
—que quiere decir en griego
maleficiosa hechicera— [63]

terror of those deserts and Circe of those mountains —
which in Greek means an "evil-doing witch" —

The five senses who form Ulysses' company of "vasallos" are
converted by her into animals. In the end, however, he is saved
by Entendimiento who persuades him to board the "nave de la
Iglesia" and to escape the realm of sin with the aid of Penitencia. [64]

---

[62] *Los encantos de la culpa,* in *Obras completas,* ed. A. Valbuena Prat
(Madrid, 1952), III, 407a.

[63] *Encantos,* 414.

[64] The extent to which ancient navigators lent themselves to the adapta-
tion of Christian themes is exemplified by Calderón's *auto sacramental El
divino Jasón.* Jason is divinized into the figure of Christ, and the Argonauts
become the disciples. The voyage takes them to the earth, which is called
Nuevo Mundo and *Islas Bárbaras,* where Christ retrieves the Golden Fleece,
that is, a soul. Christ borne on a ship on his voyage into the world is also
the theme of a German Christmas song by D. Sudermann (1608):

We note in this and other treatments of the geographical quest the persistent reappearance of paradise or a *locus amoenus,* which is either the goal of the quest in the Christian *peregrinatio* of St. Brendan, or an incidental encounter in non-ascetic voyages such as *Os Lusíadas.* Common to both cases, however, is the awareness of the recovery of a remnant of a lost era. Thus, e.g., in *La Gerusalemme liberata* the nymphs compare the condition of their island to that of the Golden Age of man:

> Questo è il porto del mondo; e qui è il ristoro
> de le sue noie, e quel piacer si sente
> che già senti ne' secoli de l'oro
> l'antica e senza fren libera gente. [65]

> This is the world's haven; here is relief for its vexations.
> Here one feels the delights which during the Golden Age
> the ancients enjoyed with unbridled freedom.

This comparison touches on an often-repeated topic of the period, as it is also echoed, e.g., by Don Quijote in his speech on the Golden Age:

> Dichosa edad y siglos dichosos aquellos a quien los anti-
> guos pusieron nombre de dorados, y no porque en ellos
> el oro, que en nuestra edad de hierro tanto se estima, se
> alcanzase en aquella venturosa sin fatiga alguna. . . . [66]

> Happy the age and happy those times which the ancients
> called "Golden" not because one could obtain effortlessly
> that gold which in our Age of Iron is so esteemed. . . .

For Don Quijote the present times are the "edad de hierro," a result of the degeneration from the "edad de oro," a decline

---

> Es kommt ein Schiff geladen
> bis an sein höchsten Bord
> trägt Gottes Sohn voll Gnaden,
> des Vaters ewigs Wort.

A ship is coming, laden to the highest deck; it is carrying God's gracious Son, the Father's eternal Word.

[65] Tasso, *La Gerusalemme,* XV, 63.

[66] *Don Quijote de La Mancha,* ed. Martín de Riquer (Barcelona, 1944), I, 9.

whose process was accompanied by the perversion of humanity. It was to counteract this trend that chivalry was introduced:

> andando más los tiempos y creciendo más la malicia, se instituyó la orden de los caballeros andantes. [67]

> as time went on and malice grew, the order of knights was established.

PEREGRINATIO and the Mythical Origin of Navigation

Don Quijote, who is well versed in the literature of the *antiguos,* refers here to the pagan legend of creation, well known since the Middle Ages through the *Metamorphoses* of Ovid. Here the effects of the Iron Age are described as follows:

> de duro est ultima ferro.
> protinus inrupit venae peioris in aevum
> omne nefas fugitque pudor verumque fidesque;
> in quorum subiere locum fraudesque dolusque
> insidiaeque et vis et amor sceleratus habendi.
> vela dabant ventis nec adhuc bene noverat illos
> navita, quaeque prius steterant in montibus altis,
> fluctibus ignotis exsultavere carinae. [68]

> The last one is the hard Iron Age. Immediately all evil bursts out in this age of baser dispositions. Modesty, truth and faith flee, and their places were taken by fraud, scheming, treachery, violence and cursed love of profit. Men now spread sails to the winds, even though the sailors did not know them well. The ships [whose wooden substance] had before stood [in the form of trees] on mountain tops, now leaped headlong into the unknown waves.

In Ovid's view the advent of the Iron Age was accompanied among other features by the inception of seafaring. Interestingly, he classifies it as a disagreeable result along with the other vices, such as *nefas, insidiae, dolus, fraus.* Furthermore he lists the

---

[67] *Don Quijote,* I, 11.
[68] *Metamorphoses,* ed. Frank J. Miller (London, 1925), Bk. I, ll. 127-134.

discovery of iron, gold and the origin of war as the other consequences of the decline:

> iamque nocens ferrum ferroque nocentius aurum
> prodierat, prodit bellum, quod pugnat utroque,
> sangineaque manu crepitantia concutit arma. [69]

> And now injurious iron, and gold, more injurious yet, had
> come forth. War comes which fights with both and brandishes clashing weapons with bloody arms.

We find a reflection of this thought in *Os Lusíadas*. Here an old man inveighs against the desire for fame that impels the seafarers to challenge the ocean. His central argument portrays man as an exile from the Golden Age, a condition effected by the fall of Adam:

> Mas ó tu geração d'aquelle insano,
> Cujo peccado, e desobediência
> Não sòmente do reino soberano
> Te pôs neste destêrro e triste ausência,
> Mas inda d'outro estado mais que humano,
> De quieta e da simpres innocência,
> Idade d'ouro, tanto te privou,
> Que na de ferro e d'armas te deitou. [70]

> Oh unhappy offsprings of that madman, whose sin and disobedience [were responsible] not only for placing you into exile from that sovereign kingdom, but also for depriving you of that superhuman condition of simple [unspoiled] innocence, [namely the] Golden Age, and condemned you to this age of iron and arms!

Man is thus in the age of iron, and consequently cursed with arms and war. Bereft of his "simpres innocência," there is no enterprise, either good or evil, which man does not dare to undertake. Indeed, it is a fate to which he is condemned:

> Nenhum cometimento alto e nefando,
> Por fogo, ferro, agua, calma e frio,

---

[69] *Metamorphoses*, Bk. I, ll. 141-144.
[70] *Os Lusíadas*, IV, 98.

Deixa intentado a humana geração.
Mísera sorte! Estranha condição! [71]

[But now] the human race leaves no undertaking untried,
however notorious or evil it may be, be it through fire,
water, heat, or cold, or the iron sword. How wretched its
lot, and how strange its condition!

Included among these enterprises is seafaring, and the old man
hurls a special curse on the man who initiated it:

Ó maldito o primeiro, que no mundo
Nas ondas velas pôs em seco lenho!
Dino da eterna pena do profundo,
Se é justa a justa lei que sigo e tenho. [72]

A curse on him who first sailed in a flimsy craft on
the world's oceans. He deserves eternal punishment in
Hell, if the just law which I follow and adhere to is
[indeed] just.

This thought is also echoed by Bartolomé de las Casas in the
Historia de las Indias (1552). Beginning his treatise with the history
of the world, he shows the initial blessed state of the first man.
Man's increasing malice, however, led him to explore the seas:

Pero creciendo cada día más y más la humana industria,
curiosidad y también la malicia, y ocurriendo eso mismo
a la vida frequencia de necesidades o de evitar males, o
buscando el reposo de adquirir bienes, huyendo peligros ... fue necesario abrirse las puertas que la oscuridad
del olvido y neblina de la antigüedad cerradas tenía, des-
cubriendo lo ignoto y buscando noticia de lo que no se
sabía.
Y puesto que aqueste discurso parece haber sido el
camino de los hombres, por el cual gentes a gentes se han

---

[71] *Lusíadas*, IV, 104.

[72] *Lusíadas*, IV, 102. See also Critilo's invective in Gracián's *El criticón*:

O tirano mil vezes de todo el ser humano aquel primero que con
escandalosa temeridad fió su vida en un frágil leño al inconstante
elemento" (I, 1).

Oh scourge of the whole human race, he who with shameful audacity first entrusted his life to the inconstant element in a fragile
craft!

> manifestado, por que éstas pueden, suelen ser y son las
> causas que por natura mueven los apetitos a dejadas sus
> proprias patrias, en las ajenas ser peregrinos. [73]

> But as man's ingenuity, curiosity and malice grew from
> day to day, and, as it often happens in life, because of
> necessity, or to avoid hardships, or to seek the opportunity
> for acquisition while avoiding dangers ... it was neces-
> sary to open the doors shut by long oblivion and the
> mists of age, and to discover and seek out information
> about the unknown.
>
> This course seems to have been the direction of man's
> path, whereby people became mutually acquainted. These
> tend to be, and [in fact] are, the reasons which incite
> their longing to leave their lands, to be strangers abroad.

Thus man, propelled by sinful *malicia* and *apetitos,* became an
exile, a *peregrino* on the sea.

A similar view is held by Samuel Purchas, who in twenty
volumes compiled accounts of voyage from the mythical ones of
Aeneas and Solomon to the voyages of discovery of his day under
the title *Purchas His Pilgrimes* (1625). He finds that man in his
original blessed state was made by God the Lord of creation,
endowed with the mastery over all beings and elements:

> The Sea covereth one halfe of this Patrimony of Man,
> whereof God set him in possession when he said, replenish
> the earth and subdue it, and have dominion over the fish
> in the Sea; and over the fowl of the Aire, and over every
> living thing that mooveth upon the Earth. [74]

But when man by the act of original sin usurped his privileges,
he forfeited his mastery over all creation, including his power
over the sea, which as a result of the Fall now showed its hostility
against man in the form of the Great Flood:

---

[73] Las Casas, *Historia,* 18a. See also *El criticón:*

> En vano la superior atención separó las naciones con los montes y
> los mares si la audacia de los hombres halló puentes para trasegar
> su malicia" (I, 1).

> In vain the Supreme Guardian separated the nations with mountains
> and oceans; for man's audacity found bridges over which to dis-
> seminate malice.

[74] Purchas, *His Pilgrimes,* I, 45-46.

And when the Sea had, as it were, rebelled against rebellious Man, so that all in whose nostrils was the breath of life, and all that was in the dry Land died, yet then did it all that time indure the yoke of Man, in that first of ships the Arke of Noah (p. 46).

Only by building this his first ship could man meet the challenge of the seas and, in fact, regain his dominion over it:

Thus should Man at once loose halfe his Inheritance, if the Art of Navigation did not inable him to manage this untamed Beast, and with the Bridle of the Winds, and Saddle of his Shipping to make him serviceable (p. 46).

For Purchas, then, the rise of the "Art of Navigation" was not so much an effect of man's Fall as it was a remedy to combat the results of the Fall. Seafaring holds for him less of a stigma than for Ovid, Camões and Las Casas, but it is a reminder nevertheless of man's loss of innocence. As a result of the Fall man became a pilgrim on earth, "[Man], preferring the Creature to the Creator, ... therefore is justly turned out of Paradise to wander, a Pilgrime all over the World." [75] The nature of seafaring is such that it recalls the condition of this pilgrimage:

---

[75] Purchas, I, 136. What applied to general original sin could also apply to individual sin. In that case the *peregrinatio* was likewise viewed as an effect of sin. This is illustrated by Mendes Pinto in his classic account *Peregrinação* (1614). In it he relates his twenty-one year odyssey in the Orient in the course of which he suffered numerous shipwrecks, and was sixteen times sold as a slave. Yet he accepts his fate as an expiation for his sins and thanks God in conclusion:

Eu dou muytas graças ao Rey do Çeo, que quis que por esta via se cumpriesse em mim a sua diuina vontade, e não me queixo dos Reys da terra pois eu não merecy mais por meus grandes peccados.

I give many thanks to the King of Heaven who wanted His Divine will to manifest itself in this manner, and I do not accuse the earthly kings, because for my great sins I did not merit otherwise.

(See *Peregrinação*, ed. A Casais Monteiro [Lisbon, 1962], II, 681).

The professed experiences of Mendes Pinto, though severe, were not uncommon in this time of hectic navigational activity, as is testified by the numerous accounts of shipwrecks recorded in the famed *História Trágico-Marítima*. One such victim, the padre Gaspar Affonso, tells of his errant adventures in Asia and America following the sinking of his ship. He too

> At sea ... no Earth is seene, only the Heaven and the inconstant shifting Elements, which constantly put us in minde of our Pilgrimage, and how neere in a thin ship, and thinner, weaker, tenderer body we dwell to death, teaching us daily to number our days. [76]

Thus a general sense of sin and guilt were the heritage with which the men of the fifteenth and sixteenth century took to the sea. The men who actually undertook the voyages would not, of course, be stopped by the thought of this heritage. Seafarers are of necessity overwhelmingly men of action, characterized by an excess rather than a deficiency of optimism. On the other hand, the societies which sent them found reason enough to regard the ventures with mixed feelings, as is borne out e.g. by the invective of the old man in *Os Lusíadas*. There is a similar critique in Góngora's *Soledades* where an old *serrano* upon seeing the soggy clothes of the *peregrino* inveighs against the originator of seafaring:

> ¿Cuál tigre, la más fiera
> que clima infamó hircano,
> dió el primer alimento
> al que —ya deste o aquel mar— primero
> surcó, labrador fiero,
> el campo undoso en mal nacido pino? (I, ll. 366-371)

> What tiger — the most vicious that ever infested the Hircanian region with its cruelty — nursed the one who, like a fierce plowman, furrowed the field of waves of this or that sea with his ill-omened pine[-craft]?

---

characterizes his unfortunate wanderings as "tão larga e trabalhosa peregrinação." Moreover, he is willing to admit that his hardships were meritorious, suggesting thereby that they served as an ascetic expiation:

> E assim quero eu contar parte desta peregrinação tão nova, e de si tão meritoria, a qual foi Nosso Senhor servido dar fim depois de tres annos e desanove dias, começada para um Oriente, e proseguida por tantos Occidentes.

> Therefore I want to narrate part of my noteworthy and meritorious pilgrimage, which our Lord consented to terminate after three years and nineteen days, and which began in the Orient and continued in many western regions.

See *Relação da viagem e successo que teve a não S. Francisco ... no anno 1596*, in *Historia Tragico-Maritima*, ed. Bernardo Gomes de Brito (Lisbon, 1905), XVIII, 8.

[76] Purchas, I, 56.

The first navigators were the Argonauts and the men of Aeneas; yet while they were sensible enough to confine their voyages in the enclosed Mediterranean, today's seafarers, moved by cupidity, venture into the unknown:

> Piloto hoy la Codicia, no de errantes
> árboles, mas de selvas inconstantes,
> al padre de las aguas Oceäno
>
> . . . .
> dejó primero de su espuma cano
>   sin admitir segundo
> en inculcar sus límites al mundo. [77]

Today, Cupidity, [having become the] pilot of not [merely a few] errant tree[-crafts], but of [veritable] unstable forests [of ships, has been the] first to leave, [as an effect of the unprecedented traffic], the ocean, the father of the waters, grizzled with his [own] foam, without allowing any second [competitor to surpass it in] imposing its [navigational] contours upon the globe.

Cupidity is also the charge of the French essayist Cholières, who in 1585 accuses the Spaniards in particular for their hunger for gold:

> Telle ardeur de jour à autre sur-croissait, et ne peut estre temperée par les longues et perilleuses allées qu'il falloit entreprendre, ny par l'apprehension des calamitez que souffrent journellement les pèlerins de l'ocean. Ce feu de rapine dorée les vous forcena de telle sorte que ce fut à l'envy à qui premier auroit la corde au col et seroit lientié de s'aller pendre et precipiter dans les gouffres et horribles ondes de la mer. [78]

Such passion [for the gold] increased day by day and could not be tempered by long and perilous journeys which they had to undertake, nor by the fear of disaster which the pilgrims of the ocean suffered daily. This fire of rapacious [passion for] gold deranged them so intensely that they seemed to vie as to who would first

---

[77] *Soledades*, Pt. I, ll. 403-405, 409-412.

[78] Nicolas de Cholières, "De l'Or et du fer," *Oeuvres de Cholières*, ed. Tricolet (Paris, 1879), p. 19.

have the rope around his neck, and be bound to throw himself into the abysmal and terrible waves of the sea.

Unhappily it is precisely the search for gold which leads the *pèlerins de l'ocean* to discover new lands:

> Pour qui nous recherchons, outre la Trapobane,
> A travers mille mers, une autre Tramontane;
> Et despitans la rage et des vents et des eaux,
> Découvrons chaque jour des mondes tous nouveaux. [79]

> For which [gold] we search beyond Trapobana, across a thousand seas, for yet another Tramontana. And defying the turmoil and the winds and the waters we discover every day completely new worlds.

The greed for gold, too, is responsible for the sins perpetrated in its name:

> Pour qui, las! si souvent le frère vend son frère,
> Le père vend son fils, et le fils vend son père. [80]

> For which [gold] a brother sells his brother, a father sells his son, and a son sells his father.

Cholières did not intend to condemn gold *per se* but its misuse in human hands. Gold had its virtues if utilized for lofty causes — a fact that was recognized by the idealists of the age. Columbus for example was borne along, among other things, by the desire to find gold which could be utilized to finance a decisive Holy War against Islam. [81] Samuel Purchas thought similarly when he named King Solomon the prototype of the pilgrim-navigators. Solomon, he held, sailed to Orphir and despoiled it of its gold in order to adorn his temples. Since by this act he served God rather than his own desires he did a just deed. [82]

One perceives the underlying dilemma of these debates, namely to what use the treasures of the newly found lands, and for that

---

[79] Cholières, p. 23.

[80] Cholières, p. 23.

[81] Joachim Leithäuser, *Worlds Beyond the Horizon*, trans. H. Merrick (New York, 1955), p. 30.

[82] Purchas, *His Pilgrimes*, I, 1-37.

matter the lands themselves, should be put. The idealists, notably Columbus, held that any material exploitation should benefit spiritual ends, i.e., the enhancement of Christianity. The Church too envisioned a spiritual exploitation of the new worlds through missionary activity. But the realities were known to be different, and they weighed heavily on the consciences of such sensitive men as Las Casas. The Spanish crown, which prided itself as the champion of Christianity, can be credited with at least attempting a balance between material and spiritual exploitation, of trying to make the new world a spiritual as well as a geographical part of its domain. [83] This aim was essentially a medieval one, for in Europe of the Middle Ages the geographic and the spiritual universe were identical, as Dante testifies by his scheme of the world. But this integration was the fruit of centuries of work by the Church. At the end of the fifteenth century the known geographic world suddenly grew immensely larger than the spiritual one. As the men sailed to the new worlds the enormous distances not only separated them from their physical homelands but also threatened to divorce them from the moral laws of the Christian civilization. As a result they behaved irresponsibly; their instincts of greed, unchecked by reason, made them lust after the gold and made them "pèlerins de l'océan," strangers, wanderers, slaves of their own baser motives. They behaved, in short, like strangers at their worst. It is fitting therefore that the minds of the era should, out of all the characteristics of the seafarer, pay such heed to his status as a stranger. His peculiar attributes, such as the moral instability, the physical dangers, or the incredible loneliness which in Os Lusíadas makes Vasco da Gama characterize his band as "mísera gente peregrina" — these qualities intrigued poets and philosophers alike for their unusual human drama. As a theme these qualities possessed additional attraction by their resemblance to the Christian peregrinatio of life on earth. Such was the powerful suggestive effect of the theme that not only could the action of seafaring inspire a literary, philosophical, or religious idea, but the idea in turn could inspire the action as

---

[83] Otis Green, Spain and the Western Tradition (Madison and Milwaukee, 1965), III, 49-52.

illustrated by the following concluding example of the Pilgrim Fathers.

PEREGRINATIO *and the Settling of North America*

In his account of the Mayflower project, William Bradford, the leader of the "Pilgrims," states that they would have liked to remain in the Dutch city of Leyden where they found temporary shelter after their exodus from England. But in a country ruled by Catholic Spain their freedom of worship was endangered and they decided to leave:

> So they lefte that goodly and pleasante citie, which had been ther resting place near 12. years; but they knew they were pilgrimes, and looked not so much on those things but lift up their eyes to the heavens, their dearest cuntrie, and quieted their spirits. [84]

Here the Christian concept of *peregrinatio* most directly attains a concrete form by triggering an historical event. Later generations honored the accomplishment, with the result that the motif was included in the American anthem, where America is characterized as the "land of the pilgrim's pride." [85]

---

[84] William Bradford, *History of Plymouth Plantation, 1606-1646,* ed. W. T. Davis (New York, 1908), p. 79. One of the children born during the voyage was named Peregrine. Peregrine is also the name of a boy in Richard Brome's comedy *The Antipodes* (1635). Through excessive reading of the travel books the boy goes mad but is cured by being taken on an imaginary voyage to the "antipodes," a trip which is also called a "pilgrimage." See *The Antipodes,* in *Dramatic Works of Richard Brome* (London, 1873), III, 248.

[85] The term "pilgrims" as applied to the Mayflower group was officially revived in 1793 in a memorial sermon by one Rev. Chandler Robbins. The notion of "Pilgrim Fathers" stems from Daniel Webster's address at the bicentennial celebration in 1820 (Encyclopedia Britannica).

Chapter II

A METAPHOR OF PROBLEMATIC LOVE

Peregrinatio Amoris

We noted in the preceding chapter that the *peregrinatio* of geographical discovery was motivated by a host of impulses. People committed themselves to hazardous voyages impelled by such motives as the search for paradise, the lure of gold, or the desire for freedom of conscience. As the voyages became the subject of literary elaboration so, too, the motives which were attributed to them became more elaborate and more fictional. Thus in *Las soledades* the youthful *peregrino* puts to sea because of his despair over his unreciprocated love. When he suffers shipwreck he arrives at a pleasant pastoral environment where he finds a measure of consolation for his heartache.

Antonio Vilanova, in his study of the *peregrinatio* of the lovelorn youth, has found that it forms part of a tradition of Italian and Spanish Renaissance poetry. His findings confirm

> the existence in literature of a fictional character, who is a model of the errant lover, who is fed up with the world and overcome with disillusionment, who searches for consolation and oblivion in the solitude of nature. This character, which appears in an uninterrupted succession throughout the Renaissance until his reappearance as the protagonist of Góngora's *Soledades,* is the pilgrim of love (*peregrino de amor*). [1]

---

[1] Translated from Vilanova, "El peregrino de amor," p. 460.

Vilanova's conclusions are convincing. This present study, therefore, is not intended to retrace his steps but rather to explore a question which Vilanova's conclusions pose. In all of the examples in which the figure of the *peregrino de amor* occurs, the type of love described is either unhappy or at least problematic. Now, poets in general are inclined to portray unhappy rather than happy love, and one is compelled to ask why. Could the frequent appearance of the metaphor of *peregrinatio* which accompanies this problematic love shed light on this question? As we have seen, *peregrinatio* is a highly complex concept, yet it possesses a precise interior logic which consists in the hardships that may or may not be meritorious, and in the desire for paradise. One would expect that the same interior logic may be found in the type of love which it describes. In this way the metaphor of *peregrinatio* could serve as an instrument of cognition to be used as a means of probing the anatomy of problematic love as portrayed in literature. To test the usefulness of this instrument will be the purpose of this chapter.

We propose to begin our analysis with a passage from Cervantes' *Don Quijote*. In Part II, Chapter 12, the two protagonists Don Quijote and Sancho overhear the Caballero del Bosque lamenting his fate as a lover in the following manner:

> ¡Oh la más hermosa y la más ingrata mujer del orbe! ¿Cómo que será posible, serenísima Casildea de Vandalia, que has de consentir que se consuma y acabe en continuas peregrinaciones y en ásperos y duros trabajos este tu cautivo caballero?

> Oh, most beautiful and ungrateful woman in all the world! How can it be possible, most serene Casildea de Vandalia, that you permit your captive knight to be consumed and to perish in continuous wanderings and harsh and trying hardships?

The Caballero del Bosque is, of course, an impersonation by the Bachiller Sansón Carrasco designed to persuade Don Quijote to return home. His impersonation is successful, because the substance and the form of his discourse are intimately familiar to Don Quijote from his knowledge of the books of chivalry. It characterizes the view of courtly love which Don Quijote himself holds and which he is trying to relive in concrete form. For he, too, imagines himself to be driven to despair by the disdainful attitude of his lady. He, too, has attempted to regain her favors by undergoing the "trabajos" of a penitential self-effacement in imitation of Amadís de Gaula's penitence at Peña Pobre; and at every point of his journey he hopes to gain a glimpse of her. And finally, he too labels his quest for a revived chivalry a "peregrinación." [2]

The Provençal Troubadours: Distant Love

Don Quijote, then, believes himself to be faithful epigone of the courtly lovers whom he so intensely admires. His belief is justified, because the view of love as a hardship is the underlying characteristic of courtly love, as the Provençal troubadours testify. One of the works which treat the theme comprehensively in both epic and lyric form is the anonymous and fragmentary romance *Flamenca* (ca. 1240-1250). In it a nobleman named Guillems makes his way southward to Provence in order to court the beautiful and renowned Flamenca, who has been compelled to marry the unloved Archimbaus. The latter, suddenly overcome by an inordinate and unjustified jealousy, has imprisoned her in a tower under the closest surveillance imaginable. Yet by means of an immensely laborious and elaborate scheme Guillems succeeds in communicating his love to Flamenca, a love which she accepts and which they eventually consummate. A knightly tournament at the court of Archimbaus, at which Guillems distinguishes himself, concludes the fragment.

Because Guillems' love is adulterous, he is forced to outwit and outmaneuver the defensive measures of the *gilos*, the jealous husband. He does so by obtaining a tonsure and by serving masses at the chapel which Flamenca is allowed to attend. He communicates with her at the giving of the *pax* by softly saying

---

2   Ella ha sido de las más suaves y dulces que en todo el discurso de nuestra peregrinación nos ha sucedido. (II, 58.)

This [adventure] has been one of the most delightful and most agreeable that has happened to us in the whole course of our wanderings.

one word when he takes the missal back from her. At the giving of
the *pax* of the next mass she responds in a few syllables. This
dialog continues until after a period of three months they have
exchanged a twenty-word message. Understandably, the waiting
period causes Guillems immense suffering with all the attendant
symptoms of love-sickness, the *mals d'amor*. [3]

Yet it is this purpose which outweighs the importance of his
hardships, and which makes them indeed pleasurable:

> Que mis mals d'amor mals non es
> Ans mi plas mais que nulla res (vv. 2050-2051).

For my love hardship is not a hardship [at all]; rather it
pleases me more than anything else.

Guillems' venture is thus motivated by an intense devotion, whose
tone is set in the very outset of his undertaking:

> Partitz soi de tota ma gent
> E vengutz sai en est païs
> Aisi con estrainz pellegris
> Que negus hom no m'i conois (vv. 2041-2044).

I have left all my people and have come to this land just
like a strange pilgrim, for no man knows me there.

Comparing himself to a pilgrim he points out that he has forsaken
the comfort and familiarity of home and exchanged them for the
hardships and the anonymity of an alien country. Just as a devout
pilgrim would make these sacrifices in order to visit the shrine
of his avowed saint, so Guillems makes them in order to win
the love of a lady; and as the former eventually arrives at his
devotional goal, in the same way the latter attains his objective
after considerable hardships.

The figure of the pilgrim, then, is symptomatic of Guillems'
arduous approach to love. That it is also an apt device with
which to circumcribe this type of love may be judged by the
fact that it is also utilized by the twelfth-century poet Jaufré
Rudel in his celebrated poem "Lanquan li jorn son lonc en
may...." Here the poet portrays himself, in the fullest flower of

---

3 *Flamenca*, in *Les Troubadours* (Paris, 1960), v. 3314.

springtime, overcome by an insatiable yearning for his *amor de lonh*, his lady-love in a distant land. He wishes he could be near her, be seen by her, and communicate his love to her. To accomplish this he could not imagine a better means than becoming a pilgrim and lodging with her:

> Ai! car me fos lai pelegris,
> Si que mos fustz e mos tapis
> Fos pels sieus belhs huelhs remiratz!
> Be·m parra joys quan li querray,
> Per amor Dieu, l'alberc de lonh:
> E, s'a lieys platz, alberguarai
> Pres de lieys, si be·m suy de lonh:
> Adoncs parra·l parlamens fis
> Quan drutz lonhdas er tan vezis
> Qu'ab bels digz jauzira solatz. [4]

Alas! Would that I were a pilgrim there so that my staff and robe would be gazed on by her beautiful eyes. It will seem to me a great joy when I can ask her, for the love of God, for [hospitality in] the distant hospice, and if it please her, I will lodge near her, though I am from afar. Then my speech will seem fine to her, when the distant lover will be so nearby that he may enjoy her solace with lovely words.

Her house, he says, would be the most luxurious hospice for a pilgrim that he can imagine:

> en tals aisiz,
> Si que la cambra e·l jardis
> Mi resembles tos temps palatz! [5]

---

[4] Jaufre Rudel, "Lanquan li journ son lonc en may...," *Nouvelle Anthologie des troubadours*, ed. Jean Audiau (Paris, 1928), p. 26.

[5] Carl von Krauss, editor of *Deutsche Liederdichter des 13. Jahrhunderts*, notes in German courtly love poetry the motif of the lover who enters the chambers of his beloved in the disguise of a pilgrim. As an interesting variation on the motif I cite the following poem by Gotfrit von Nifen. Here a pilgrim seeks to enter the hospice of *Minne*, 'love in the abstract':

> Vom Walhen fuor ein pilgerîn
>   mit sînem kötzeline.
> zerhouwen wâren im die schuo;
>   er was sô rehte fine.
> er bat der hereberge in der minne.
> 'ja enist er niht guot pilgerîn'
>   sprach der wirt 'vil leit ist er mir hinne.'

in such a hospice the chamber and the garden seem to me at all times a palace.

To be near her the poet would gladly suffer all manner af hardships, and would not even shun captivity by the Sarracens:

> Tant es sos pretz verais e fis
> Que lay el reng dels Sarrazis
> Fos hieu per lieys chaitius clamatz!

Her merit is so true and fine that there, in the kingdom of the moors, I would for her be called a captive.

Yet paradoxically, while he is willing to accept such extreme sacrifices, he complains that the distance is insurmountable:

> Mas non sai quoras la veyrai,
> Car trop son nostras terras lonh:
> Assatz hi a pas e camis.

But I do not know when I will see the [distant love], for our lands are too far apart, there are too many steps and roads [separating us].

Evidently he considers this distance a far greater obstacle than any imaginable hardship, an obstacle which he feels he cannot possibly overcome, which is beyond his control. In the last stanzas he suggests that the distance may be less a geographical one than a psychic one. His love can never be requited:

> 'Waz hilfet iuwer metti gân
> un iuwer venjen suochen,
> daz ir des armen pilgerîns
> hie inne niht went ruochen?'
> er bat der hereberge in der minne.

A pilgrim came from his pilgrimage, [dressed] in his garb. His shoes were tattered; he was a truly fine [pilgrim]. He asked for lodging in [the hospice of] love. "But you are not a good pilgrim," the innkeeper said, "you are a great nuisance in here." "What good is it," [replied the pilgrim] "that you go to Mass, and beseech [God] with kneeling, if you do not take care of this poor pilgrim in here [as a true Christian should]?" He asked for lodging in [the hospice of] love.

Deutsche Liederdichter (Tübingen, 1952), ed. Carl von Krause, I, 121.

Mas so qu'ieu vuoill m'es atahis,
Totz sia mauditz lo pairis
Que·m fadet qu'ieu non fos amatz.

But what I want is forbidden to me. Cursed be the godfather who bewitched me so that I should not be loved.

Because he has been doomed from birth never to have his love returned, no amount of personal exertion can win his lady's love. This recognition sets him apart from Guillems, because the latter's primary obstacle was the *gilos*, whom he outmaneuvered through wit and endurance, an effort which eventually obtained for him the object of his love. Flamenca herself does not resist his advances, because according to the Ovidian love principle which pervades the work, a prolonged refusal of the lover is judged unbecoming of a woman. [6] Thus she remains within Guillems' reach and even permits herself to yield her body to him. For Guillems, then, the hope for attainment is an essential ingredient of his *peregrinatio*, even though it may be interrupted periodically by moods of despair. In Rudel's poem, on the other hand, hope is absent because the poet's destiny prevents the requital of his love. His lady remains unattainably aloof. Since therefore his *peregrinatio* promises no success, he abandons it as pointless. It is reduced to the status of an unrealized wish-dream, as indicated by the optative clause "car me fos lai pelegris."

Yet, paradoxically, the poet relishes his love in spite of its hopelessness:

[6] Trop es domna de mala guisa
Si dousors de prec non l'aguisa;
E trop es cala causa dura
Cui douzors de prec non madura
Trop es cel cors durs e gilatz
Et en si meseis aturatz,
Quan douzors de prec i deisent,
Sin non desgela mantenent (vv. 2903-2910).

That woman is of bad disposition who does not heed the sweetness of entreaties. That object is hard which is not mellowed by the sweetness of entreaties. That person is too hard and frozen and too self-regarding who does not melt when she is touched by the sweetness of entreaties.

> Car nulhs autres joys tan no·m play
> Cum jauzimens d'amor de lonh.

For no other loves so pleases me as the enjoyment of distant love.

The phrase "amor de lonh" is ambiguous. On the one hand, it may designate the woman:

> [Dieus] ... mi don poder,
> . . . .
> Qu'ieu veya sest' amor de lonh,
> Veraymen, en tals aizis.

May God ... give me the power that I may see this distant love ... in such a place.

On the other hand, "amor de lonh" may also signify the very state of being in love, describing a specific type of love, one that is content to limit itself to mere adoration from a distance, content to love hopelessly and unrequitedly. When therefore the poet asserts that the "amor de lonh" affords him supreme pleasure: ("nulhs autres joys tan no·m play"), he acknowledges that he is in love not only with a woman, but with love itself. He is stepping back to contemplate in perspective his own state of being in love, and from this contemplation he derives his pleasure. [7] His consciousness of love has thereby attained a second dimension.

---

[7] We find an echo of this feature in Oscar Wilde's novel *The Picture of Dorian Gray:*

> Someone has killed herself for love of you. I wish that I had ever had such an experience. It would have made me in love with love for the rest of my life. The people who adored me ... have always insisted on living on.

([New York, 1964], Ch. VIII.) Here the expression "to be in love with love" signifies the intensity of the affection. It is that consuming passion which Denis de Rougemont characterizes as a persistent phenomenon in *Love in the Western World:*

> To love love more than the object of love, to love passion for its own sake, has been to love to suffer and to court suffering all the way from Augustine's *amaban amare* down to modern Romanticism.

(Trans. Montgomery Belgion [New York, 1965], p. 52.) St. Augustine, in fact, suggests that his "love of love" already existed before he even had an opportunity to focus it on someone. Speaking in his *Confessions* (Bk. III, Ch.

It has been compounded and intensified in a measure which a simple requited love could not have effected.

The DOLCE STIL NOVO *and Its Successors: Platonic Love*

The understanding reached by Rudel, then, is that the most intense and lasting love is fundamentally a hopeless one, an endless *peregrinatio* which does not bring the lover closer to the beloved. This feature was also recognized by the spiritual inheritors of the troubadours, the poets of the *dolce stil novo*, who elaborated the concept of disembodied love with an unprecedented refinement. Their most renowned student, Petrarch, also employs the motif of the pilgrimage to express his devotion towards the woman, as in the following sonnet:

> Movesi il vecchierel canuto e bianco
> del dolce loco ov'à sua età fornita
> e da la famigliola sbigottita
> che vede il caro padre venir manco:
>
> indi traendo poi l'antico fianco
> per l'estreme giornate di sua vita
> quanto più po col buon voler s'aita,
> rotto dagli anni e dal cammino stanco;
>
> e viene a Roma, seguendo 'l desio,
> per mirar la sembianza di colui
> ch'ancor lassù nel ciel vedere spera:

I, in *PL*, XXXII) of his arrival in Carthage in the time before his conversion, he comments:

> Nondum amabam, et amare amabam, et secretiore indigentia oderam me minus indigentem. Quaerebam quod amarem, amans amare, et oderam securitatem, et viam sine muscipulis, quoniam fames mihi erat intus ab interiore cibo, teipso, Deus meus, et ea fame non esuriebam.

> I was not in love yet, and yet I loved to love, and with a more secret kind of want I hated myself for wanting so little. I sought about for something to love, loving to love, and I hated security and roads without snares in them: all because I hungered for an inward food — You, my God — although it was not that kind of hunger that made me crave.

Because this kind of love is so detached from its object, it can be readily redirected to another object or goal, even to God. After his conversion his strongest goal is God, who becomes the receptacle of his passionate energy.

> così, lasso, talor vo cercand'io,
> Donna, quanto è possibile in altrui
> la disiata vostra forma vera. [8]

The poor old man, grizzled and white, leaves the sweet place where he has passed his years, and his dismayed family which sees its dear father failing.

Then, dragging his aged limbs through the last days of his life, he takes whatever courage he can muster, [though] broken by the years and weary of wandering;

And he comes to Rome, pursuing his desire, to see the likeness of Him, Whom he hopes to see in Heaven once more.

So, alas, do I sometimes, as much as possible, look for your desired true form in others.

Like a feeble old man undergoing the inappropriately extreme exertion of a pilgrimage to Rome, the poet finds himself searching for a semblance of his lady. The hardships which each suffers are out of proportion for the resources of each—the physical ones of the old man, and the psychic ones of the poet. Each is therefore making a supreme sacrifice. Nevertheless the analogy remains incomplete. For the old man will very likely reach Rome by merely sustaining his efforts and maintaining his direction. As for the goal of his journey—Rome and the desired object of worship contained in it—he can confidently expect it to be there, because Rome is a permanent reality. Moreover he can expect to be received readily, because, as one of the spiritual focal points of Christendom, Rome is accustomed to play host to pilgrims. On the other hand, the poet's success in finding his lady is less certain. In the concluding lines of the sonnet he reports himself as still searching. But despairing of his inability to find her he deviates from his goal of attaining her and instead limits himself to a mere searching of a semblance of her in others: "vo cercand'io / ... quanto è possibile in altrui / la disiata vostra forma vera." He is losing direction; his pilgrimage has thus degenerated into an aimless wandering and must be judged a failure. Like Rudel, Petrarch had to recognize that a love pilgrimage has

---

[8] Francesco Petrarca, *Rime,* ed. Siro Attilo Nulli (Milano, 1956), Sonnet XVI, p. 10.

value only if one is assured of his arrival at the object of devotion; yet, like the former, he continues loving a woman who would never return his love.

After Laura's sudden death in 1348 the last remnant of his hope is dashed. If he were to see her now it would only be in Heaven. In Sonnet CCCII he presents such a dream vision. Yet upon waking he ruefully notes how the vision escapes him:

> Deh perché tacque ed allargò la mano?
> ch'al suon de' detti sì pietosi e casti
> poco mancò ch' io non rimasi in cielo.

> Alas! Why did she go silent and release hy hand? For at the sound of such compassionate and chaste words I very nearly stayed in Heaven.

He realizes that this journey of his soul toward Heaven was an impossible fiction which would not afford him consolation. For such a movement would require an act of Christian faith. Dante, as we shall see later, had been able to commit himself to such a course of action. Petrarch, who was a less firm believer, shunned it. His despair over Laura's death is greater than his hope of seeing her in Heaven either now or after death. Since he is not, however, prepared to abandon the thought of his love, the despair will remain with him, and the remainder of his life will be characterized by it. In the Canzone CCCLX he sums up the suffering and the restlessness which will constitute his life under the influence of love. Writing about love, he says that it

> Cercar m' à fatto deserti paesi,
> fiere e ladri rapaci, ispidi dumi,
> dure genti e costumi
> ed ogni error che' pellegrini intrica.

> [It] has caused me to seek out deserted lands, wild beasts and rapacious robbers, bristly underbrush, harsh people and customs, and all the vagaries in which a wanderer gets involved.

His life is consumed in an incurable restlessness; he is driven about like a *pellegrino*, a wandering stranger. In his *peregrinatio* of love he no longer maintains any direction, because the destination, Laura, is impossible to reach. It is not therefore the attractiveness of a goal which compels him to wander about, but only the desperation of his agitated spirit which is stricken by love. In short, the motivating force of his *peregrinatio* is no longer Laura, but he himself. Petrarch himself is its protagonist. His love, then, is self-oriented. [9]

We noted earlier that Rudel's *amor de lonh* represents the condition of a lover who is in love with love itself. His love is no longer dependent for its existence on the lady's requital of it. The lover himself therefore is the sole participant in the love affair. It too is a self-oriented love. Similarly Petrarch's love rests entirely on himself, because Laura does not participate in it. One notes that in the introductory sonnet of the *Canzoniere*, where Petrarch states the purpose of the work, any mention of Laura's person is absent. Instead, he asserts that the purpose of his poems is primarily to describe the "sospiri ond'io nudriva il core," his own lamenting reaction to his own unhappy love. Even in his lament about Laura's death (sonnet CCLXVII) he is unable to forego a thought about himself:

> Oimè il bel viso, oimè il soave sguardo,
> oimè il leggiadro portamento altero!
>
> . . . .
>
> Per voi convèn ch' io arda e 'n voi respire,
> ch' i' pur fui vostro, e, se di voi son privo,
> via men d' ogni sventura altra mi dole.
> Di speranza m' empieste e di desire
> quand' io parti' dal sommo piacer vivo:
> ma 'l vento ne portava le parole.

> Alas! [Gone is] the beautiful face; alas, [gone is] the gentle look! Alas! [Gone is] the easy, dignified posture! . . .

---

[9] Maurice Valency, in his study of Renaissance love poetry, finds this self-oriented love to be characteristic of all the *stilnovisti* in general:

> It is obvious that the poet is concerned chiefly with states of mind, his own mind, ont with objective things. The beauty of the lady is a reflection of the poet's desire; her cruelty is a projection of his aggression. The poet describes himself first and always. Ultimately, this poetry has little to do with women.

See *In Praise of Love* (New York, 1961), p. 210.

> It is only right that I burn for you and breathe in you,
> for I was indeed yours, and since I am [now] deprived
> of you [I am so grieved that] I have little mind for any
> other misfortune.
> You thrilled me with hope and desire when I took leave
> of my supreme pleasure. But the wind carried the words
> away.

This passage is not only a mourning about Laura's departure, it is also a statement of an immensely personal loss. In the moment of greatest grief his self-consciousness never leaves him, and it permeates the lament with a strong element of self-pity.

Yet this self-pity is only an extension of the self-concern that characterized Petrarch's love even before Laura's death. When she vanishes from the scene, the intensity of his love remains nearly constant, because the attitude of the subject *io* remains the same. [10] The impression which his poetry produces is correspondingly one of a pervasive monotony, because the love affair is presented to the reader from an unchanging focus throughout the 366 poems.

A sampling of post-Petrarchan love poetry will demonstrate that this self-oriented love concept is perpetuated by Petrarch's successors. In the following examples I cite a selection to which Vilanova too alludes, namely a *canzone* of Pietro Bembo's work, *Degli Asolani* (1505), "Lasso, ch'i' fuggo e per fuggir non scampo...." Here the poet portrays himself in the condition of a lover who, like Petrarch, wanders about the countryside in solitary despair:

---

[10] Denis de Rougemont has noted this feature of self-love in his analysis of the "myth" of Tristan:

> The love is *mutual* in the sense that Tristan and Iseult "love one another," or, at least believe that they do. Certainly their mutual fidelity is exemplary. But *unhappiness* comes in, because the love which "dominates" them is not a love of each other as that other really is. They love one another, but each loves the other *from the standpoint of self and not from the other's standpoint*. Their unhappiness thus originates in a false reciprocity, which disguises a twin narcissism. So much is this so that at times there pierces through their excessive passion a kind of hatred of the beloved.

(See *Love in the Western World*, pp. 54-55). Although Tristan's love shares the self-concern of Petrarchan love, it differs decisively by the fact that this self-concern applies to both, the man and the woman. In Petrarchan love, on the other hand, the man is the only active participant and the self-orientation applies only to him.

> Se in alpe odo passar l'aura fra 'l verde,
> sospiro e piango e per pietà le cheggio,
> che faccia fede al ciel del mio dolore;
> se fonte in valle o rio per camin verde
> sento cader, con gli occhi miei patteggio,
> a farne un del mio pianto via maggiore;
> s'io miro in fronda o 'n fiore,
> veggio un che dice: o tristo peregrino,
> lo tuo viver fiorito è secco e morto.
> E pur nel penser porto
> lei, che mi diè lo mio acerbo destino;
> ma quanto più pensando io ne vo seco,
> tanto più tormentando Amor ven meco. [11]

When I hear in the mountains the breeze passing through the greenery, I sigh and weep, and I ask it to kindly give testimony to Heaven of my grief. When I hear a spring or a river descend into the valley, I cause its path to swell with the tears of my eyes; and when I gaze at the leaves or flowers I see one that says: oh sad wanderer, your [once] flourishing life is dried up and dead. And then I bear in my thoughts her who imposed this bitter destiny on me, but the further I pursue my thoughts, the more Love, torturing me, comes with me.

The suffering lover perceives the compassion of nature, which reminds him of his miserable condition as a *peregrino*. His love is unfulfilled; there is thus no hope for any progress on his *peregrinatio*. His reaction is one of extreme self-pity. He expresses his craving for compassion in words addressed to other unhappy lovers:

> Deh, si pietà vi punge,
> date udienzia insieme a le mie pene (p. 372).

You there, if you are touched with pity, lend an ear to my grief!

The lover is above all aware of his own person, and his self-concern overshadows his preoccupation about the actual object of his love, the woman.

---

[11] Pietro Bembo, *Degli Asolani,* in *Prose e Rime,* ed. Carlo Dionisotti (Torino, 1960), pp. 371-372.

Don Quijote *and Problematic Love*

Returning now to *Don Quijote* we recall how the Caballero del Bosque portrayed himself to Don Quijote as being engaged in "continuas peregrinaciones." That is, having lost the favors of Casildea his "peregrinación" has become aimless and directionless. Don Quijote is likewise engaged in a "peregrinación," that of knight-errantry. He, too, pursues a love affair, because it is a mandatory activity for every knight:

> Yo soy enamorado, no más de porque es forzoso, que los caballeros andantes lo sean; y siéndolo, no soy de los enamorados viciosos, sino de los platónicos continentes" (II, 32).

> I am in love, if only because knights-errant are obligated to be; and being so, I am not one of those depraved lovers, but of the continent platonic sort.

He calls his love Platonic, in contrast to the purely sensual, *vicioso* love. Moreover, he asserts that he loves solely for the purpose of complying with the demands of chivalry. To this end the woman serves only as a means, her participation in this love affair is not needed, because the love affair is sustained entirely by Don Quijote himsel.

His love is hopeless and will never be fulfilled as the omen tells him, "no la has de ver en todos los días de tu vida" (II, 73). His *peregrinatio*, then, is a futile one. In fact, of course, Dulcinea does not for all practical purposes exist, so that his love was doomed to hopelessness in the first place. Nor does she need to exist. For, according to the principles of Platonic love which Don Quijote so explicitly professes to follow, the woman in her fleshly form is not the goal of love; rather she serves as the starting point for the lover's intellectual ascent towards a transcendental ideal of beauty and perfection. In the last analysis, then, it is not an affair between a lover and a woman, but between the lover and the intellectual ideal;[12] that is, the importance of the

---

[12] We find an echo of this kind of love in a sonnet by Elizabeth Barrett Browning:

lover outweighs that of the woman. Ultimately, the response of the woman, although desirable, is not needed. The lover is likely to continue his gestures in spite of her refusals. It is by its very nature that Platonic love permits the kind of self-orientation that we have already observed in Petrarch.

Nevertheless, even the Platonic lover was allowed the pleasure of contemplating the physical beauty of a woman, if only to give an impetus to his intellectual contemplation. Don Quijote lacks even this aid; he is able to proceed directly to worship an ideal of perfection without requiring the concrete presence of the woman. His love, then, illustrates the epitome of disembodied love; it represents the Platonic principle carried to an abnormal extreme. Don Quijote is, of course, not normal; he is mad. And it is only his madness which allows him to forego the tangible evidence of Dulcinea and yet at the same time not discontinue his devotions. It is thus with the ingredient of madness that Cervantes was able to illustrate the problematic nature of Platonic love. In all of his writings he endorses it explicitly for its concom-

---

If thou must love me, let it be for nought
Except for love's sake only. Do not say
"I love her for her smile — her look — her way
Of speaking gently, — for a trick of thought
  That falls in well with mine, and certes brought
A sense of pleasant ease on such a day" —
For these things in themselves, Beloved, may
Be changed, or change for thee — and love, so wrought,
  May be unwrought so. Neither love me for
Thine own dear pity's wiping my cheeks dry, —
A creature might forget to weep, who bore
  Thy comfort long, and lose thy love thereby!
But love me for love's sake, that evermore
Thou mayst love on, through love's eternity.

She exhorts the lover to detach his love from its physical causes, i.e., to disembody it in accordance with the Platonic principle. Instead she wants him to love her for the sake of the abstract ideal, "for love's sake." She also adds one more admonishment, namely that he not love her merely to satisfy his own self ("Neither... for / Thine own pity's wiping my cheeks dry"). As a woman she cannot bear the thought of being merely an object used for the man's self-satisfaction, however disembodied the affection may be. It appears then that the idea of self-oriented, hopeless love is far less congenial to the mind of a woman than to the mind of a man, because it does not call for the woman's participation. "Sonnets from the Portuguese," XIV, *The Poetical Works of Elizabeth Barrett Browning* (London, 1890), IV.

itant virtues. Yet, if it was carried to a logical extreme, as is done by Don Quijote, it required for its maintenance a spiritual tenacity, an *idée fixe* of a magnitude which the ordinary lover could not muster.

The Byzantine Romance: Meritorious Hardships in Love

The inordinate feature of Don Quijote's love is elucidated by a comparison with another *peregrinatio* of love, that of Pánfilo in Lope de Vega's novel *El peregrino en su patria* (1604). Pánfilo is planning to marry his sweetheart Nise, but the family negotiations break down. In despair, he abducts her, and both travel incognito throughout the countryside. He becomes separated from her on repeated occasions, suffers imprisonment, is nearly executed, and becomes in a myriad of other adventures until both he and Nise find their way home, where they are joined in marriage.

Pánfilo's name is not revealed until the novel is well under way. Instead, he is known only as *el peregrino*. Like Don Quijote, he too is engaged in an eventful *peregrinatio*, a wandering search for his beloved. However, for Don Quijote the search is as hopeless as is his love; he will never experience the presence of Dulcinea, let alone her requital of his love. Pánfilo, on the other hand, is assured of Nise's love; his separation from her is not caused by her rejection of him, but by outside circumstances to which both of them are subjected with equal rigor. Both face similar and often common trials, and both call themselves *peregrinos*. Both vow and practice chastity. In the face of their fate, then, they are essentially equal. On the other hand Don Quijote's love is characterized by an essential inequality, because it requires the submission of the lover to the beloved.

Another difference consists in the duration of the *peregrinatio*. Don Quijote's wanderings lead to no result, and like Petrarch's *peregrinatio* they could potentially continue endlessly. Pánfilo, however, eventually attains the goal of his *peregrinatio*, his reunion with Nise. Though he may despair at times of the lack of progress in his journey, it is only a temporary hopelessness; success finally crowns his persistence. When he and other couples are united after similar fates, Lope exclaims:

> "Dichosos peregrinos de amor, que ya en su patria des-
> cansan, cumplido el voto." [13]

> Fortunate pilgrims of love, who are now resting in their
> homeland with their vows completed!

Pánfilo is a *peregrino de amor* whose exclusive devotion to his
love is manifest in his name (Pan-, 'all,' -filo, 'love'). "La patria"
may mean on the one hand his homeland; in an extended sense
it may also refer to the place where his happiness is located:

> dondequiera que está el bien, como Apuleyo y Cicerón
> escriben, es la verdadera patria (pp. 190-191).

> wherever the good is, as Apuleius and Cicero write, there
> is the true homeland.

Since his greatest good, "el bien," consists in Nise, his "patria" is
wherever Nise is. In the face of this reality the geographical
meaning of "la patria," his hometown, loses importance, for without
Nise it becomes meaningless to him. He abandons his home rather
than Nise. Not until he is given permission to marry her does he
agree to return. When he does so, the two meanings of "la patria"
have become united.

The elaborate plot of *El peregrino en su patria* is modeled on
a prose genre that enjoyed immense popularity among Lope's
contemporaries, the Milesian tale. Because the most popular
versions originated in the Byzantine period, they became also
known as the Byzantine romances. All of them treat the fate of
couples who left their homeland because contrary circumstances
prevented their marriage. They lose each other repeatedly, undergo
numerous adventures, but in the end they return and marry.
As Theagenes in the *Historia Aethiopica* (3. cent. A.D.) indicates,
love is the primary motive for the wanderings; for its sake
the lovers endure voluntary exile. [14] In Achilles Tatius' novel,

---

[13] Lope de Vega Carpio, "El peregrino en su patria," in *Colección
de las obras sueltas* (Madrid, 1776), V, 461.

[14] Theagenes characterizes himself and Carichlea as he implores Carichlea's companion Calasiris for aid:

Leucippe and Clitophon (2. cent. B.C.), Leucippe reminds her lover that only because of him she endures such hardships, "For you I left my mother and took up the life of a wanderer (διά σέ τὴν μητέρα κατέλιπον καὶ πλάνεν εἱλόμην), for you I suffered shipwreck and fell into the hands of pirates...." [15] As the insistent διά σὲ 'for you' indicates, it is an exclusive devotion to their love which has compelled her to leave home, a love that was stronger than any enticement of comfort which the parental home could have offered her.

Love, then, is the motive for the wanderings in the Byzantine romance. This motive also appears in Boccaccio's novel *Filocolo* (ca. 1336). Here Florio, the son of a Spanish king, loves Biancofiore, a girl living at the court under the tutelage of the royal family. Through intrigues Biancofiore is incriminated, and the enraged king sells her as a slave to a travelling merchant. Florio sets out after her, traversing the realms of the Mediterranean until he finds her. When his father dies, he returns and assumes the throne with her.

σῶζε ... ὦ Καλάσιρι, ξένους καὶ ἀπόλιδας ἱκέτας πάντων ἀλλοτριωδέντας, ἵν' ἐκ πάντων μόνους ἀλλήλους κερδήσωσι.

Oh Calasiris, save us strangers and homeless suppliants, so that [although we are] dispossessed of everything, we may [at least] gain each other!

(*Heliodori Aethiopica*, in *Scriptores Graeci et Latini*, ed. Aristides Colonna [Roma, 1938], p. 135.) We note that Heliodorus uses the word ξένος, 'stranger, wanderer,' which Fulgentius already translated as *peregrinus*. In a sixteenth-century Italian translation of this passage it is similarly translated as *pellegrino*:

O Calasiride... salua i pellegrini scacciatti de la patria loro tuoi familiari; salua coloro, che hanno abbandonato ogni altra cosa, acciò guadagnino solamente di potersi godere insieme.

(*Historia di Heliodoro delle cose Ethiopiche*, trans. Leonardo Glinci [Venezia, 1586], p. 154.) A Spanish translation of 1587 by Fernando de Mena similarly uses the word *peregrino* in this passage:

¡Oh buen Calasiris, salvad estos peregrinos y estos pobres sin ciudad ni habitación alguna, privados de todas las cosas, sólo porque de todas ellas se puedan ganar el uno al otro!

See *Historia Etiópica de los amores de Teágenes y Cariclea*, ed. Francisco López Estrada (Madrid, 1954), p. 168.

[15] Achilles Tatius, *Leucippe and Clitophonte*, ed. and trans. S. Gaselee (London and New York, 1917).

Asked by foreigners to describe himself and his activity, Filocolo answers:

> Io mi son un povero pellegrino d'amore, il quale vo cercando una mia donna a me con sottile inganno levato da miei parenti; e questi gentili uomini i quali con meco vedete, per loro cortesia nel mio pellegrinaggio mi fanno compagnia: e il mio nome e Filocolo." [16]

> I am a poor pilgrim of love, who is [wandering about], searching for his lady, whom my parents took away from me with subtle ruse; and these gentlemen whom you see with me are accompanying me on my travels out of kindness; and my name is Filocolo.

Florio labels himself a *pellegrino d'amore* [17] and the wandering in search of his sweetheart a *pellegrinaggio*. The degree to which he identifies himself with his cause is indicated by his name, which Boccaccio defines as *Fatica d'amore*, the 'hardship of love.' [18] Florio's love is a painful experience, marked by hardships and temporary despair. As Boccaccio points out, this painfulness is not the exclusive experience of Filocolo, but is rather characteristic of, if not a necessity of, love:

---

[16] Giovanni Boccaccio, *Il Filocolo,* ed. Salvatore Battaglia (Bari, 1938), p. 292.

[17] He says that he changed his name when he became a *pellegrino d'amore:*

> ... io mi chiamo Florio, e per tema della fama del mio nome, divenuto pellegrino d'amore, in Filocolo il trasmutai (p. 442).

> ... my name is Florio, but for fear of my name's reputation I have changed it to Filocolo, having become a pilgrim of love.

[18] Filocolo e da due greci nomi composto, da 'philos' e da 'colon'; 'philos' in greco tanto viene a dire in nostra lingua quanto 'amore' e 'colon' in greco similmente tanto in nostra lingua resulta quanto 'fatica': onde congiunti insieme, si puo dire, trasponendi le parti, Fatica d'Amore.

> The name Filocolo is composed of two Greek words: *philos* and *colon; philos* in our language means approximately "love" and *colon* "hardship"; so the two [taken] together mean "hardships of love."

(Boccaccio, p. 274). Boccaccio is in error here. He was, in fact, referring to the Greek κόπος Accordingly, the editor of the 1828 edition corrected the title in the first of the two volumes to *Filocopo.* The second volume, curiously, retains the title *Filocolo.* See Boccaccio, *Opere volgari,* VII-VIII (Firenze, 1828).

I corpi si dovevano allontanare ma le menti con più sollecitudine si dovevano far vicine. Ni una cosa e più desiderata que quella che è impossibile, o molto malegevole ad avere" (p. 69).

The bodies should be far apart, but the minds should approach each other even more fervently. Nothing is more desirable than the impossible or the very arduously attainable.

The more difficult an object is to attain, the more desirable it becomes. The greater the physical distance that separates the two lovers ("le corpi"), the more intense are the efforts of the minds ("le menti") to seek union. Distance, in short, heightens the consciousness of love. Boccaccio thus advocates difficult love, distant love ("i corpi si dovevano allontanare") for the same reason for which Jaufré Rudel eulogized "amor de lonh."

This plea distinguishes *Filocolo* from the Byzantine romances, in which the struggle of the lovers is directed merely to the achievement of union. The innumerable adventures are regarded as nothing more than hateful obstacles that must be overcome. In *Filocolo* we find a similar struggle, but we also find that the author reflects on the value of the struggle itself. *Filocolo* thus displays a meditative awareness of love of a magnitude unmatched by the Byzantine novel of antiquity, an awareness that is rooted in the tradition of the troubadours.

This focus on the merits of the struggle and hardships of the *peregrinatio* also characterizes *El peregrino en su patria:*

Quien no ha peregrinado, ¿qué ha visto? quien no ha visto ¿qué ha alcanzado? quien no ha alcanzado ¿qué ha sabido? ¿y qué puede llamar descanso, quien no ha tenido fortunas o por la mar, o por la tierra? pués como Ovidio dice: No merece las cosas dulces quien no ha gustado de las amarguras; ni ha tenido regalado día en la patria, quien no ha venido de larga ausencia a los brazos de sus amigos (p. 453).

He who has not travelled, what has he seen? He who has not seen, what has he accomplished? He who has accomplished nothing, what has he learned? And what can he call rest, who has never [experienced the vicissitudes

of] fortune on sea or on land? For as Ovid says, he who
has not tasted bitterness does not deserve the sweet
things. Nor has he who never returned into the arms of
a friend after a long absence had a truly pleasant day in
his homeland.

Lope's understanding resembles Boccaccio's: the hardships of the
peregrinatio render the amenities of live even more pleasant; one
appreciates something more highly if one experiences the opposite
("las cosas dulces ... las amarguras"). The enjoyment of the
"patria" is enhanced through the experience of exile. The *peregrino's* temporary absence from his sweetheart will intensify his
joy over the final reunion with her in the "patria."

The same emphasis on the hardships is also evident in Cervantes' novel *Persiles y Sigismunda* (1617). Here the prince Persiles
elopes with his sweetheart Sigismunda to avoid losing her to his
brother who wants to marry her. To keep Sigismunda away from
his brother, Persiles persuades her to leave home under the pretext
of undertaking a pilgrimage to Rome. They undertake it together,
and in spite of occasional separations they remain together. They
too are engaged in a *peregrinatio,* not only because they are
pilgrims going to Rome, but because they are forced to leave their
"patria" for the sake of their love. [19] When at last they arrive in
Rome they meet Persiles' dying brother, who bestows Sigismunda
on Persiles.

The hardships of their *peregrinatio* have not been futile. As
Sigismunda asserts, they have rather intensified their love:

> Sola vna voluntad, ¡o Persiles!, he tenido en toda mi vida,
> y essa aurá dos años que te entregué, no forçada, sino
> de mi libre aluedrío; la qual tan entera y firme está agora
> como el primer día que te hize señor della; la qual si es
> possible que se aumente, se ha aumentado y crecido entre
> los muchos trabajos que hemos passado (II, 203).

> In all my life, oh Persiles, I have had only one love, and
> it has been two years now since I offered it to you out of

---

[19] Persiles characterizes himself and Sigismunda as "miserables peregrinos, desterrados de su patria." See Miguel de Cervantes, *Los trabajos
de Persiles y Sigismunda,* ed. R. Schevill and A. Bonilla (Madrid, 1914),
I, 104.

free choice, without compulsion. And it is as undivided and firm now as on the day you first took possession of it. And if it is possible for it to increase, it has increased and grown with the hardships we have endured.

Sigismunda thus focuses on their difficulties and hardships *(trabajos)* and realizes their beneficial effect on love. That Cervantes himself recognized this effect is evident from the title of the work, *Los trabajos de Persiles y Sigismunda.* Love proves itself most effectively under the influence of adversity and hardships, which the *peregrinatio* provides in abundance. The environment of the *peregrinus* changes constantly, a factor which renders his condition essentially unstable. As his impressions of the environment change, so also the perception of the world is subject to alteration. Of his ideas and beliefs only the firmest ones survive. What holds true for the condition of the *peregrino desterrado* also applies to life in general; it is part of the human condition. [20] If changes of mind and heart can result from a temporary *peregrinatio,* how much more so will they occur in life itself:

> Como están nuestras almas siempre en continuo moui-
> miento, y no pueden parar ni sossegar sino en su centro,
> que es Dios, para quien fueron criadas, no es maraui-
> lla que nuestros pensamientos se muden (II, 5).

> Since our souls are always in a state of agitation and can-
> not stop and calm down until they reach their central
> [resting place], which is God — for whom they were
> created — it is not surprising that our ideas should change
> too.

Not until after death is tranquillity possible. Restlessness and instability of the soul are the rule of life. Life thus becomes a

---

[20] Clodio excuses the exaggerated claims of hardships that are frequently made by the "desterrados" returning from Turkish captivity, because he finds that the dangers to which life as a whole is subject may be more incredible than any single experience:

> aunque parezca que cuentan impossibles, a mayores peligros está
> sugeta la condición humana, y los de vn desterrado, por grandes
> que sean, pueden ser creederos.

continuous challenge to the eternal values of the soul for as long as the soul is exiled in its *peregrinatio* on earth.

PEREGRINATIO AMORIS *and* PEREGRINATIO VITAE

It is not surprising, then, that the *peregrinatio* of love should become closely associated with the *peregrinatio* of life. This association emphatically pervades *El peregrino en su patria,* where each of the five books concludes with a Biblical quotation alluding to the *peregrinatio* of life, such as:

> Audientes igitur semper, scientes quoniam dum sumus in corpore, peregrinamur a Domino. [21]

> Therefore we are always confident, knowing that, whilst we are at home in the body, we are absent from the Lord.

That is, for as long as the soul is in the body it is a *peregrinus,* a 'wandering exile,' temporarily estranged from God. Only in Heaven will it find its true home, its "patria."

For Pánfilo's *peregrinatio* of love Lope thus found a convenient analogy which enabled him to combine a topic of considerable interest to his contemporaries with an important Christian maxim. He conforms thereby to the esthetic principle of *delectare et prodesse,* so dear to the official thought of the Counter Reformation. But it also characterizes the kind of assimilation and alteration to which both Lope and Cervantes subject the Milesian tale by broadening the significance of the *peregrinatio.* [22]

> although it may seem that [the exiles] tell impossible things, they can be believable, considering to how much greater perils the human condition [as a whole] is subject. *Cervantes,* Persiles, II, 5.

[21] 2. Cor. 5, 6. See Lope de Vega, *El peregrino,* p. 189.

[22] In the Prólogo to the *Novelas ejemplares* Cervantes makes the well-known claim of the excellence of the forthcoming *Persiles y Sigismunda,* "te ofrezco los Trabajos de Persiles, libro que se atreue a competir con Eliodoro, si ya por atreuido no sale con las manos en la cabeça" (ed. Schevill-Bonilla [Madrid, 1922], I, 23). From the standpoint of the Counter Reformation his romance would indeed outdo Heliodorus', for by broadening the concept of *peregrinatio* he brought the Milesian tale up to date:

> Cervantes had adopted the Byzantine novel as a model; however, by making pilgrims *(peregrinos)* out of his protagonists he surmounted, with a stroke of the pen, the [merely] anecdotal signi-

In fact, the newly attributed meaning of *peregrinatio* proved to be a productive theme in itself, as exemplified by Baltasar Gracián's *El Criticón* (1651). Here Critilo is prevented by intrigues from marrying his beloved Felisinda. Returning to Europe from India, he sets out in search of her traversing various countries in the company of the savage Andrenio. His search is a *peregrinatio* of love. Yet, as Critilo's journey progresses, his concern for Felisinda recedes. It is overshadowed by another activity, the observation of humanity. From his observations he derives moral conclusions, "critical" judgments for the benefit of his pupil Andrenio. The nature of his *peregrinatio* is finally clarified for him when he attends a philosophical discussion of the famous minds of the period, such as Barclay, Marino, *et al.*:

> En vano, ¡o peregrinos del mundo, passajeros de la vida! os cansáis en buscar desde la cuna a la tumba esta vuestra imaginada Felisinda, que el uno llama esposa, el otro madre, ya murió para el mundo y vive para el cielo. Hallarla heis allá, si la supiéredes merecer en la tierra. [23]

> In vain, oh pilgrims of the world, passers-by of life, do you exhaust yourselves from the cradle to the grave in search for your imagined Felisinda, which one calls his spouse, the other his mother; she already died for the world and now lives for Heaven. You will find her there, if you know how to merit her on earth.

A radical change is evident. Felisinda is now no longer portrayed as being of flesh and blood; she is "imaginada," and is likely to be found only in Heaven. Correspondingly, Critilo's *peregrinatio* is no longer one of love. It is now a *peregrinatio* of life; Critilo and Andrenio are "peregrinos del mundo, passajeros

---

ficance of the adventures of his models. For the adventures and changes of action acquire a new and enhanced meaning by being encased in a love pilgrimage (*peregrinación de amor*) which is at the same time an allegory of human life.

Translated from J. B. Avalle-Arce's introduction to his recent edition of the *Persiles* (Madrid, 1969), pp. 24-25.

[23] Baltasar Gracián, *El criticón*, ed. M. Romera-Navarro (Philadelphia, 1940), Pt. III, Ch. 9.

de la vida." It marks the change from a purely personal *peregrinatio* to one which is common to all of humanity, a change which the author indicates by calling the two in a fraternal manner "nuestros peregrinos." Felisinda similarly appears no longer as a person, but as a symbol containing the abstract concept of true happiness, of happiness sought by all mankind, but not found on earth:

> No tenéis que cansaros en buscar la felicidad en esta vida, milicia sobre el haz de la tierra" (III, 9).

> You need not fatigue yourselves in searching for happiness in this life which is a struggle on the face of this earth.

Love and the Devotional Pilgrimage

Beside the *peregrinatio* of life one additional type of *peregrinatio* was developed by the Milesian tale. In *Persiles y Sigismunda* the heroine undertakes a pilgrimage to Rome in order to escape marriage with Persiles' brother and to preserve her love for Persiles. Although initially it served as a pretext, the pilgrimage is carried out with full devotion once it is resolved upon. In *El peregrino en su patria* Pánfilo and Nise travel in pilgrims' clothes, since they were a convenient disguise for travellers in need of anonymity. Occasionally the motive for such a disguise was love, as it was, for example, in the celebrated case of Margarite d'Aubusson. [24] When Pánfilo and Nise return and are united, Lope

---

[24] Marguerite d'Aubusson used the pilgrimage as a pretext to meet Huguet de Lusignan. (See Georges Lambin, "Passionate Pilgrims," *Etudes Anglais*, XVII [1964], 458.) Instances also abound in fiction. In *All's Well That Ends Well*, Shakespeare presents the story of Helena whose husband left her shortly after their wedding. She, too, uses a pilgrimage as a pretext for searching for him ("her pretence is a pilgrimage to Saint Jaques le Grand," IV, 3). In *The Two Gentlemen from Verona*, Julia is determined to find her lover Proteus. She says that she will master the arduous search with the same tenacity with which the pilgrim strives to reach the sanctuary:

> Julia.   ... tell me some good mean,
> How, with my honour, I may undertake
> A journey to my loving Proteus.
> Lucetta. Alas! the way is wearisome and long.
> Julia. A true-devoted pilgrim is not weary

comments that they have fulfilled the vow which they had sworn
as *peregrinos de amor:*

> Dichosos peregrinos de amor, que ya en su patria descan-
> san, cumplido el voto" (p. 461).

> Fortunate pilgrims of love, who now rest in their home-
> land, with their vows completed.

Not until the pilgrims have arrived at the object of their devotion
can they allow themselves to be at rest.

This devotional attitude, then, makes the pilgrimage inherently
suitable to characterize the nature of love. A medieval Anglo-
Norman treatise of love, *La Clef d'amours,* asserts this fact explicitly:

> Amour nous a si doctrinez
> que touz i sommes enclinez
> et les fames comme les hommes:
> dex soit quelz pelerins nous sommes.
> Mes entre nous a tel distance
> que l'omme de parler s'avance,
> et la fame, je l'ose dire
> plus couvertement le desir.
> L'omme doit le premier preer
> et enchancier et suppleer. [25]

> Love has so indoctrinated us, that we are all disposed to
> it, women as well as men. God knows what kind of pil-
> grims we are. But between us is such distance, that the
> man comes forward to speak, and the woman, I dare say,

To measure kingdoms with his feeble steps;
Much less shall she that hath Love's wings to fly,
And when the flight is made to one so dear,
Of such divine perfection, as Sir Proteus (II, 7).

[25] *La Clef d'amours,* ed. Auguste Doutreport (Halle, 1890), vv. 560ff.
Washington Irving, in his collection of short stories entitled *The Alhambra,*
wrote *The Legend of Price Al Kamel; or The Pilgrim of Love,* which concerns
a Moorish prince who goes in search of a distant princess. "I am a pilgrim
of love, and seek but to find a clue to the object of my pilgrimage." Like
a pilgrim Al Kamel, too, took a vow: "You behold before you a votary of
love, who would fain seek counsel how to obtain the object of his passion."
See *The Alhambra* (New York, 1884), p. 142.

covertly desires it. The man should be the first to entreat, to [en]chant, and to supplicate.

Men and women, indoctrinated by love, are inclined towards each other. They are attracted by each other in the same manner in which pilgrims are attracted by their devotional shrine. The great distance which separates them must be covered by the man, who, like a penitential pilgrim, prays ("preer") and supplicates ("suppleer"). Thus, even in their semantic detail, the terms of the pilgrimage are highly adaptable to descriptions of the attitudes which are at play in the process of a love affair.

This feature is also exemplified by the play *The Lover's Progress* (ca. 1623) by Beaumont and Fletcher. Here Calista is forced to refuse the wooings of Lisander because she is married to Cleander. Lisander, in turn, like a "poor mortif'd Pilgrim" [26] supplicates her with the devotional phraseology of a pilgrim:

> Your servant, your most obedient slave (adored Lady)
> That comes but to behold these eyes again,
> And pay some Vows I have to sacred Beauty,
> And so pass by; I am blind as ignorance,
> And know not where I wander, how I live,
> Till I receive from their bright influence
> Light to direct me, for Devotions sake,
> You are the Saint I tread these holy steps to (V, 105).

Lisander's pilgrim-like devotion is ultimately rewarded, for when Cleander dies in a scuffle, the widowed Calista accepts her lover.

In another play by the same authors, *The Pilgrim* (1621), the lover Pedro dresses in pilgrim's clothes to be near his unattainable and adored sweetheart Alinda. To hide his identity he lets another fellow-pilgrim speak to Alinda:

> ALINDA. You are pilgrims, is't not so?
> OLD PILGRIM. We are, fair saint. May heaven's grace surround you; may all good thoughts and prayers dwell upon you. [27]

---

[26] Francis Beaumont and John Fletcher, *The Lover's Progress*, in *Works* (Cambridge, 1908), V, 102.

[27] John Fletcher, *The Pilgrim* (Philadelphia, 1811), p. 13. This is an altered version by John Dryden. In the original by Fletcher this particular

He, too, compares the relationship between the lover-admirer and the woman to that of the pilgrim and the saint, as does also Alinda's servant Juletta when she espies the handsome Pedro:

> Holy pilgrims they seem to be. What pity 'tis that handsome young fellow should undergo so much penance. Would I were the saint he makes his vow to; I'd soon grant his request, let him ask what he would (p. 13).

Shakespeare, too, makes use of this terminology in his plays, as he does, for example, in his most intense tragedy of love, *Romeo and Juliet* (1595):

> ROMEO. If I profane with my unworthiest hand
> This holy shrine, the gentle sin is this:
> My lips, two blushing pilgrims, ready stand
> To smooth that rough touch with a tender kiss.
> JULIET. Good pilgrim, you do wrong your hand too much,
> Which mannerly devotion shows in this.
> For saints have hands the pilgrims' hands do touch,
> And palm to palm is holy palmers' kiss.
> ROMEO. Have not saints lips and holy palmers too?
> JULIET. Ay, pilgrim, lips that they must use in prayer.
> ROMEO. O! then, dear saint, let lips do what hands do:
> They pray. Grant thou, lest faith turn to despair.
> JULIET. Saints do not move, though grant for prayers' sake.
> ROMEO. Then move not, while my prayers' effect I take.
> Thus from my lips, by thine, my sin is purg'd. [28]

In the coy exchange of affectionate terms Romeo is called a "pilgrim," and Juliet the "saint," whom he must entreat by prayer. This is the first meeting of the two lovers within the play. It is therefore an important meeting, because it indicates the auspices under which the love affair begins, and under which their relationship begins to form. This relationship, then, is defined by analogy with that of the pilgrim and the saint. It is noteworthy that in Italian the word *romeo* is synonymous with *pellegrino*, 'pilgrim.'

---

passage is not contained. Dryden's addition reveals the continuing interest which this theme enjoyed even during the later English baroque.

[28] I cite from *The Oxford Shakespeare*, ed. W. J. Craig (New York, 1936), Act I, sc. 5.

Since the origin of the story of *Romeo and Juliet* is traceable to an Italian source, it is very likely that Shakespeare was familiar with the meaning of the name in either its Italian form or its Latin translation of *romeus* that was employed by his contemporary Arthur Brooke in a verse epic, *Romeus and Juliet* (1562). Neither Brooke nor the author of the Italian source story, Luigi da Porto, exploits the meaning of the name. [29] On the other hand, judging by the above quoted passage, Shakespeare seems to have been aware of its significance and willing to exploit it for the purpose of underlining Romeo's exclusive devotion to love.

The figure of the pilgrim symbolizes intense religious devotion. When, therefore, a writer describes a love affair in the terminology of a pilgrimage, he shows a desire to dignify love, to endow it with a degree of importance which is normally attributed to religion. One wonders, therefore, how Christian thought reacted to the abundant homage which was paid to the cause of idealized love by poets and philosophers. Criticism was, in fact, not lacking, as is testified by the example of the *caballero* Vivaldo in *Don Quijote*, who looks askance at the knights-errant of literature who invoke the spiritual assistance of their ladies rather than that of God before starting dangerous ventures:

----

[29] The story of Luigi da Porto is entitled *Novella novamente ritrovata d'un Innamoramento: Il qual successe in Verona nel tempo del Signor Bartholomeo de la Scala: Hystoria Iocundissima.* See the photographic reproductions of the editions of 1535 and 1539, ed. Maurice Jonas (London, 1921). The names of the protagonists are Romeo Montecchi and Giuletta Capelletti.

Da Porto pretends to have received the story from a soldier. Interestingly enough, the name of the soldier is Peregrino; among his other characteristics is the outstanding tendency to be in love in spite of his 50 years, "forse più di quello, che agli anni suoi si sarebbe convenuto, innamorato sempre" (Da Porto, ed. of 1539, p. 24).

Whether Shakespeare himself wished to call attention to the significance of the name cannot be said with complete certainty. Juliet's remarks in Act II, Scene 2, would seem to negate that assumption:

> What's in a name? that which we call a rose
> By any other name would smell as sweet.

Romeo concurs, saying, "Henceforth I never will be Romeo." Yet it seems that in this passage Romeo and Juliet do not so much want to deny the importance of the meanings of names. Rather, it seems, they wish to play down the awareness of the family strife. Their names identify them with

Una cosa, entre muchas, me parece muy mal de los caballeros andantes, y es que, cuando se ven en ocasión de acometer una grande y peligrosa aventura, en que se ve manifiesto peligro de perder la vida, nunca en aquel instante de acometella se acuerdan de encomendarse a Dios, como cada cristiano está obligado a hacer en peligros semejantes; antes se encomiendan a sus damas, con tanta gana y devoción como si ellas fueran su Dios; cosa que me parece que huele algo a gentilidad. [30]

One of the many features of knights-errant which I disapprove of is the fact that when they are about to undertake

---

their respective families and thereby call to mind the enmity that prevents their love. Romeo states it appropriately:

> My name, dear saint, is hateful to myself
> Because it is an enemy to thee   (II, 2).

[30] *Don Quijote*, I, 13. The substance of Vivaldo's objection also appears in the Incipit of *La Celestina*, which states that

> la comedia o tragicomedia de *Calixto y Melibea* [fue] compuesta en represión de los locos enamorados, que vencidos en sus desordenado apetito, a sus amigas llaman y dicen ser su Dios.

> the comedy or tragicomedy of Calixto and Melibea [was] composed in reproach of those maddened by love, who overcome by their inordinate desire proclaim their beloved to be their God.

(Tragicomedia de Calixto y Melibea, ed. M. Criado de Val y G. D. Trotter [Madrid, 1958], p. 18). Calixto does in fact assert: "Melibea es mi señora, Melibea es mi Dios" (p. 197). Calisto's manner of speaking, which shocks the bystanders, suggests that he regards his love for Melibea as an alternative religion:

> SEMPRONIO. ¿Tu no eres cristiano?
> CALIXTO. ¿Yo? Melibeo soy, y a Melibea adoro, y en Melibea creo, y a Melibea amo (p. 28).

> SEMPRONIO: You are not a Christian, then?
> CALIXTO: I? I am a Melibeam, and I adore Melibea, I believe in Melibea, and I love Melibea.

His death, then, would seem to be a just punishment for having chosen the wrong alternative, that is, for having used his free will to a blasphemous end. This is implied in one of the concluding verses of the work, which exhorts the reader not to imitate the love affair of the protagonists but rather to love Christ:

> Pues aquí vemos quan mal fenecieron
> aquestos amantes, huygamos su dança.
> Amemos a Aquel que espinas y lança,
> açotes y clauos su sangre vertieron (p. 302).

> Seeing how badly these lovers ended, let us avoid their [fatal] dance and love the One whose blood was spilled by thorns, lance, lashes and nails.

a great and perilous adventure in which there is evident danger to their lives, they never in the moment of attack remember to commend themselves to God as every Christian is obligated to do in similar dangers. Instead they commend themselves to their ladies with such fervor and devotion as though these were their God, a practice which, it seems to me, smells somewhat of paganism.

Vivaldo criticizes the knights for allowing, in effect, the *devoción* for their ladies to replace the more appropriate *devoción* for God. Such an act strikes him as misplaced piety because it gives the woman the appearance of a pagan rival of God.

This suspicion of a surreptitious paganism had haunted the official Church ever since, it appears, the rise of the Albigensian heresy. Perhaps the most striking testimony of this rivalry occurs in the German legend of Tannhäuser. Tannhäuser is depicted as a devotee of Venus, enjoying the delights of her love in the Venusberg. However, his overindulgence suddenly fills him with remorse, and he decides to undertake a pilgrimage to Rome in the hope of gaining absolution for what he considers his sin. But this pardon is denied to him, and in despair he returns to the Venusberg, having concluded that if he is to be barred from eternal salvation, he will seek the next best thing, perpetual pleasure in the company of Venus. [31]

Tannhäuser's dilemma consists essentially in the conflict of two devotions, one pagan, the other Christian. His homage for Christianity he expresses by his pilgrimage. When he returns to Venus he is, in effect, replacing this religious pilgrimage by a pilgrimage of love. This feature is brought out by Richard Wagned in his opera. In it Wolfram von Eschenbach addresses Tannhäuser, who has returned from his futile pilgrimage:

> Wer bist Du Pilger,
> der du so einsam wanderst?

Who are you, pilgrim, wandering in such solitude?

---

[31] In Rome Tannhäuser also takes leave of St. Mary: "Maria muoter, raine maid / ich muoss mich von dir schaiden." ("Tannhäuser," in *Deutsche Dichtung des Mittelalters*, ed. Friedrich von der Leyen [Frankfurt, 1962], p. 682.) Thus we have in the poem the opposition of St. Mary and Venus, an opposition which symbolizes the conflict of the Christian and the pagan devotion.

Tannhäuser replies that he seeks the way to the Venusberg:

> Doch such' ich wen, der mir den Weg wohl zeige,
> den Weg, den einst so wunderleicht ich fand —
> *Wolfram von Eschenbach.* Und welchen Weg?
> *Tannhäuser.* Den Weg zum Venusberg. [32]

> I am searching for someone who could show me the way,
> the way which once I found so easily ...
> *Wolfram von Eschenbach.* And which way?
> *Tannhäuser.* The way to the Venusberg.

As Wolfram testifies, Tannhäuser still bears the appearance of a *Pilger*, a 'pilgrim.' At this moment, however, he is on the way to Venus. His pilgrimage has thus been extended and perverted into a *peregrinatio* of love, of pagan love with Venus. The motif of the pilgrimage thus serves here as an instrument to contrast pagan and Christian devotion. [33]

---

[32] Richard Wagner, *Tannhäuser*, in *Dramatische Werke*, ed. Karl Reuschel (Leipzig, 1918), I, pp. 189-190.

[33] Even in the Middle Ages one could present a pilgrimage to Venus, as did Chaucer in *The Knight's Tale*. Palamon visits the temple of Venus to invoke her help in gaining the love of Emelye:

> With holy herte, and with an heigh corage
> He roos, to wenden on his pilgrimage
> Unto the blisful Citherea benigne—
> I mene Venus, honurable and digne.

(*The Complete Works of Geoffrey Chaucer*, ed. Walter W. Skeat [Oxford, 1940], pp. 63-64.) The setting, however, is pagan Greece, so that no spiritual conflict is called forth by the act of the pilgrimage.

A prominent echo of the motif of the pilgrimage to Venus may be found in a painting by Watteau which he originally named *Le Pèlerinage a l'isle de Cythère*, but which was later renamed *L'Embarcation a l'isle de Cythère*. Watteau apparently found the inspiration for this theme in a vaudeville of Dancourt entitled *Les Trois Cousines* and performed in 1700. Here some villagers dressed like pilgrims set out for the Temple of Love with these words:

> Venez a l'île de Cythère
> En pèlerinage avec nous.

> Come with us on a pilgrimage to the island of Cytheria.

See Michel Levey, "The Real Theme of Watteau's *Embarkation for Cytheria*," *The Burlington Magazine*, CIII (1961), 182.

It would have been impossible, however, for even the most zealous Church official to eradicate the concept of ideal love. Instead, Christianity made use of its challenger by channeling the devotional capacities of the pseudo-pagan lover towards its own purposes. One consequence of this attitude was the institution of Mariolatry, which arose, apparently, in answer to the Albigensian heresy. On the other hand, the love for a woman could also be employed to evoke a spiritual devotion, as exemplified by Dante. In the following sonnet in the *Vita nuova* (ca. 1293) he expresses his devotion for Beatrice:

> Oltre la spera che più larga gira,
>   Passa 'l sospiro ch' esce del mio core:
>   intelligenza nova, che l'Amore
>   piangendo mette in lui, pur sù lo tira.
>   Quando elli è giunto là dove disira,
>   vede una donna che riceve onore,
>   e luce sì che lo suo splendore
>   lo peregrino spirito la mira.
> Vedela tal, che quando 'l mi ridice,
>   io no lo intendo, sì parla sottile
>   al cor dolente che lo fa parlare.
>   So io che parla di quella gentile,
>   pero, che spesso ricorda Beatrice:
>   sì ch' io lo intendo ben, donne mie care. [34]

Beyond the sphere which gyrates most widely, passes the sigh that comes from my heart; new understanding which love weepingly instills into it, draws it upward. When it has reached the place it yearns for, it sees the woman, who is visited with honor, and so shines, that this far-travelled spirit wonders at her brightness.

It sees her in such a way that when it repeats this to me, I do not understand, so darkly it speaks to the grieving heart that makes it speak. I know that it speaks of that gentle one because it often recalls Beatrice, so that I understand it well, my ladies.

Dante himself provides us with an interpretation of the sonnet:

---

[34] Sonnet XXV, in Dante Alighieri, *Vita nuova*, ed. Michele Schevillo (Milano, 1911), pp. 279-281.

Ne la prima dico là ove va lo mio pensero, nominandolo
per lo nome d'alcuno suo effetto. Ne la seconda dico per
che va là suso, cioè chi lo fa così andare. Ne la terza dico
quello che vide, cioè una donna onorata là suso; e chia-
molo allora "spirito peregrino," acciò che spiritualmente
va là suso, e si come peregrino lo quale e fuori de la sua
patria, vi stae (p. 276).

In the first [part] I talk about the place to which my
thought goes, namely by [mentioning] the name of one
of its effects. In the second [part] I talk about the reason
why it goes up there, that is, who makes it go in such a
manner. In the third [part] I mention what it sees, that
is, a lady honored up there; and I call it "pilgrim spirit,"
because it goes up spiritually, and just like a pilgrim it
is away from its homeland.

Dante's faith convinces him that the deceased Beatrice's soul is
residing in the empyrium ("Oltre la spera che più larga gira.") In
order to reach her his "peregrino spirito" must ascend to Heaven.
His soul is thus engaged in a *peregrinatio* of love. Yet at the same
time it is performing a spiritual ascent to Heaven. It is likely that
without the lure of Beatrice this ascent would not have occurred.
A comparison with a sonnet of Shakespeare may illustrate this:

> Weary with toil, I haste me to my bed,
> The dear repose for limbs with travel tired;
> But then begins a journey in my head
> To work my mind, when body's work's expir'd:
> For then my thoughts — from far where I abide —
> Intend a zealous pilgrimage to thee,
> And keep my drooping eyelids open wide,
> Looking on darkness which the blind do see:
> Save that my soul's imaginary sight
> Presents thy shadow to my sightless view,
> Which, like a jewel hung in ghastly night,
> Makes black night beauteous, and her old face new.
>   Lo! thus, by day my limbs, by night my mind,
>   For thee and for myself no quiet find. [35]

Shakespeare's thought, like Dante's, undertakes a pilgrimage to
the vision of a woman who is absent from him. This vision occurs

---

[35] *The Oxford Shakespeare*, Sonnet XXVII, p. 1285.

to him in a period of insomnia, and the night-time pilgrimage of his mind is an extension of the physical pilgrimage which he undertakes by day. Because the woman is probably alive and still residing on earth, neither his body by day nor his mind by night needs to leave the earth. Viewed schematically, the poet's "pilgrimage" takes place on a horizontal plane. In contrast, Dante insists that the ascent of his *peregrino spirito* is a vertical displacement ("va là suso"). In its direction, therefore, Dante's *peregrinatio* of love corresponds to the *peregrinatio* of the mystic, who, by an act of self-mortification, propels his soul towards Heaven. However, while the mystic seeks Heaven and Paradise for the love of God, Dante is lured towards it by the memory of a beloved woman. The resemblance of his soul's *peregrinatio* to that of the mystic appears to be merely an incidental one; it is a likeness of form rather than of substance which receives no attention in the sonnet.

It is likely that this resemblance occurred to Dante himself at the time when he was writing, or compiling, the *Vita nuova*, and that it inspired him to extend the scope of the *peregrinatio* of love to include its counterpart, the spiritual *peregrinatio* of the soul. At the end of the work he promises an unprecedented extension of the vision. [86] The work which fulfills this promise is, of course, *La Divina Commedia* (ca. 1321).

The Goal of PEREGRINATIO AMORIS: *Paradise*

In the *Purgatorio* Dante appears as a penitent who makes his way toward Heaven along the steep arduous path of Mount

---

[86]   Se piacere sarà de colui a cui tutte le cose vivono, che la mia vita duri per alquanti anni, io spero di dicer di lei quello che mai non fu detto d'alcuna. E poi piaccia a colui che e sire de la cortesia, che la mia anima se ne possa gire a vedere la gloria de la sua donna: cioè de quella benedetta Beatrice, la quale gloriosamente mira ne la faccia di colui 'qui est per omnia saecula benedictus.'

If it should please the One for Whom all things live that my life continue for some years, I hope to say about [Beatrice] what has never been said of anyone before. And may it please Him Who is the patron of courtly love that my soul may turn to see the glory of its lady, that is, of that blessed Beatrice, who gloriously sees the face of Him Who is blessed for all times.

Purgatory. Like his fellow penitents, he too is a *peregrinus* [37] striving to reach the earthly Paradise. He too participates in the necessary ritual of purgation, by being branded on the forehead with the sign of the seven sins. And immediately before entering Paradise he too must traverse the cleansing fire which bars his way. When he hesitates Virgil encourages him,

> 'Or vedi, figlio,
> tra Beatrice e te é questo muro.' [38]

> Look, my son, between Beatrice and you is [only] this wall.

To rally Dante's resolution to proceed, Virgil chooses as the most effective means of enticement the memory of Beatrice. His success proves that the prospect of seeing her is the most powerful motivating force for Dante. It is his overwhelming desire to see her, to confirm his love, which prompts him to submit to the trials of purgation. At the same time he is being unburdened of the moral defects that plagued his conscience at the outset of the *Commedia*. It is she who draws him on this spiritual *peregrinatio*, who leads his mind on the way to God.

For Dante the attainment of Beatrice occurs simultaneously with his access to Paradise, for it is here that he meets her. This association of the beloved lady with Paradise was frequently made by courtly-love poets. A popular refrain in Old French poetry echoes this relationship:

(Dante, *Vita nuova*, pp. 282-283). Dante calls God the *sire de la cortesia*, thus symbolizing the intimate interpenetration of the ideals of courtly love and Christianity.

[37] At the foot of Mount Purgatory some fellow penitents ask for directions. Virgil replies, and at the same time identifies himself and Dante as pilgrims:

> voi credete
> forse che siamo esperti d'esto loco;
> ma noi siam peregrin come voi siete.

> Perhaps you think that we are acquainted with this place, but we are strangers [here] just like you.

See *Purgatorio*, ed. John D. Sinclair (New York, 1961), Canto II, vv. 61-63.

[38] Dante, *Purgatorio*, XXVII, vv. 35-36.

> Au Paradis, bel ami j'ai
> En m'amusant le chanterai. [39]

In paradise I have a pretty friend; I will entertain myself by singing of her.

To the contemporary audience this mention of paradise could not but evoke strong suggestions of the Christian Paradise, as is evident from the divinized version of the same refrain. Christ is pictured as the lover, residing in Paradise:

> En Paradis, bel ami j'ai,
> Eh! tres doux Dieu, quand vous verrai? [40]

In Paradise I have a pretty friend. Oh, most sweet God, when will I see you?

The beloved, who occupies Paradise, is entitled to draw her lover into her abode, as does Beatrice, who, as Dante asserts, "m'imparadisa la mia mente." [41] However, the emphasis on the specifically Christian nature of Paradise was not always strong, as seen in a poem by Ventadorn:

> Quan la douss' aura venta
> De ves nostre païs
> M'es vejaire qu'ieu senta
> Odor de Paradis. [42]

At times when the sweet breeze wafts toward our land, it seems to me as if I perceive a scent of paradise.

Here the suggestion of paradise is reduced to a mere sensory odor, an impression of the exterior qualities normally attributed to the Christian Paradise.

This emphasis on the purely sensual aspect of paradise is also present in the *Roman de la Rose,* where it serves to depict the garden of love which the dreamer enters:

---

[39] Cited from Gustave Cohen, *La Poésie en France au Moyen Age* (Paris, 1952), p. 19.

[40] Cohen, p. 20.

[41] *Paradiso,* XXVIII, v. 3.

[42] *Le Parnasse occitainien* (Toulouse, 1819), p. 5.

> Et sachiés que je cuidai estre
> Por voir en Paradis terrestre,
> Tant estoit li leus délitables. [43]

Know ye that I thought I was really in the earthly paradise, so delightful was the place.

Here too we sense an incipient dilution of the strictly Christian nature of the term paradise, wherein the Christian meaning becomes a partial one within the broader concept of a *locus amoenus*. This process continues with the advent of the Renaissance, as exemplified by Spenser's *Shepheards' Calender* (1579), where the Arcadian amenities of the pastoral world are compared to Paradise:

> O happy Hobbinoll, I bless thy state,
> That Paradise hast found which Adam lost. [44]

Spenser's own note clarifies the passage:

> A Paradise in Greeke signifieth a garden of pleasure, or a place of delights (p. 378).

In this sense the environment of nature as depicted in the Renaissance pastoral is alleged to resemble the pristine purity of the Christian Paradise or the Golden Age. [45] One might ask therefore to what extent the properties of paradise also carry over to the pastoral. The most important feature of paradise is its accessibility through a process of *peregrinatio*. Could this *peregrinatio* also form part of the pastoral myth? To examine this question we turn now to the first of the Renaissance pastorals, Jacopo Sannazaro's *Arcadia* (1502).

---

[43] Guillaume de Lorris, *Le Roman de la Rose,* ed. Francisque Michel (Paris, 1864), I, vv. 639-641.

[44] Edmund Spenser, *The Works,* ed. John Todd (London, 1877), p. 378.

[45] The term "Golden Age" also became synonymous with "Christian Paradise":

> Moreover by the golden age what other thing is meant,
> Than Adams tyme in Paradyse.

(*The XV Bookes of P. Ovidius Naso, entytled Metamorphosis* [London, 1575]). Cited from E. W. Taylor, *Nature and Art in Renaissance* (New York, 1964), p. 158.

PEREGRINATIO AMORIS *and the Renaissance Pastoral Myth*

To begin with we note that although the pastoral may resemble paradise it does not claim to be identical with it. This is evident from the complaint in which the shepherd Opico compares the present with the more glorious past. That he is referring to the Golden Age is apparent from the fact in those times there was no iron that might yield deadly weapons: "Non era ferro, il qual pur ch'oggi termini / l'umana vita." [46] The season then consisted of eternal spring with its delightful, balanced climate: "Non foschi o freddi, ma lucenti e tepidi / eran gli giorni." There existed the possibility of immortality through the process of reju-venation: "I vecchi ... con erbe incantate ingiovenivano." There was no strife among men: "Non si potea l'un uom ver l'altro irascere." Most of all, however, love was happy, and jealousy was absent:

> I lieti amanti e le franciulle tenere
> giran di prato in prato ramentandosi
> il foco e l'arco del figliuol di Venere.
>
> Non era gelosia, ma sollaciandosi
> movean i dolci balli a suon di cetera,
> e 'n guisa di colombi ognior basciandosi (p. 105).

The happy lovers and tender girls swirl from meadow to meadow, remembering the fire and the arch of the son of Venus.
There was no jealousy, instead they began with amuse-ment the sweet dances at the sound of the cither, and like doves they kissed.

However, in the pastoral milieu love is, more often than not, unhappy. It is a problematic love, [47] in which lack of requital,

---

[46] Sannazaro, *Opere*, ed. Enrico Carrara (Torino, 1952), p. 103.

[47] The problematic nature of this love is reflected in the terminology used to describe it. For the affairs of the pastoral world are governed not only by love, *amor*, but frequently also by *desamor*, the "absence of, and disinclination to, love" on the part of the beloved. Either condition involves the participants in its own form of pastoral solidarity. For just as *amor* draws couples together, so too *desamor* can effect its own form of together-ness:

misunderstandings and jealousy afflict the characters ceaselessly. Nearly all of their activity centers on a cure for their affliction, [48] or at least an alleviation, which they seek in the compassion of others, that is, by making their woes "public." [49] Not only do they receive the sympathy of their fellow shepherds but also that of

---

> El desamorado Lenio ... como vio que la pastora era tan enemiga del amor como parecía, y que tan de todo en todo con la desamorada condición suya se conformaba, determinó saber quién era y de seguir en su compañía. ...

> When the loveless Lenio ... saw that the shepherdess was [indeed] as inimical to love as she seemed to be, and that she matched his own loveless condition so completely, he decided to find out who she was and to seek her company. ...

See Cervantes, *La Galatea,* in *Clásicos Castellanos,* CLV, 80.

[48] To denote their love-sickness the victims frequently employ such terms as *mal,* 'illness,' *remedio,* 'cure,' and *medicina.*

[49] Gracioso pastor, para conocer el mal que maltrata tu vida basta oir las palabras que publica tu lengua.

> Graceful shepherd, to learn of the ailment which afflicts you it suffices us to hear the words which your tongue makes public.

(Gil Polo, *La Diana enamorada,* in *Clásicos Castellanos,* CXXXV, 39.) The desire to bare one's soul is characteristic of the shepherds. Only in the pastoral world does Sincero feel free to speak his heart, to be in effect "sincere." Here where nature is at its most perfect, the truth of the heart flourishes most easily. Montaigne, too, echoes this in the beginning of his *Essais:*

> Que si j'eusse esté entre ces nations qu'on dict vivre encore sous la douce liberté des premières loix de nature, je t'asseure que je m'y fusse tres-volontiers peint tout entier et tout nud.

> If I had been among those tribes which are reported to be still living in the sweet liberty of Nature's first laws, I assure you that I would have depicted myself completely and entirely naked.

(*Œuvres complètes,* ed. A. Armingaud [Paris, 1924], I, 1-2.) Nature in its primeval stage ("premières loix de nature") refers to the Golden Age. In Montaigne's time it was widely thought that the newly discovered savages of the New World lived in a state and in an environment which resembled closely the paradisiacal condition of Adam and Eve. This environment, Montaigne feels, would be most propitious for eliciting truths. The longing for love and truth in conjunction with a fervent belief in Nature characterize the Renaissance search for the pastoral world.

What holds true with respect to human truths may also apply to spiritual truths. This is implied in John Bunyan's *The Pilgrim's Progress,* where one of the shepherds on the Delectable Mountain is named Sincere. He and his companions sing the following song:

> Thus by the Shepherds, Secrets are reveal'd,
> Which from all other men are kept conceal'd:
> Come to the Shepherds then, if you would see
> Things deep, things hid, and that mysterious be.

nature itself, for whenever a shepherd gives voice to his unhappy
love in an extemporaneous dirge, the trees may incline towards
him and the wildlife may listen attentively. [50]

The animals are able to show such understanding because they
too are participants in the law of love which pervades the pastoral
scene. In *Arcadia* Sincero is reminded of his own love problem
when he perceives a "love-stricken" bull which refuses to graze:

> ... veggio tra i fertili campi alcun toro magrissimo ap-
> pena con le debole ossa sostinere la secca pelle, il quale
> veramente senza fatica e dolore inestimabile non posso
> mirare, pensando un medesimo amore essere a me et a
> lui cagione di penosa vita (p. 112).

> ... I see in the fertile fields a starved bull which is hardly
> able to sustain the dry skin, and I cannot look at it with-
> out immense pain and affliction, considering that the same
> type of love is the reason for the painful life of both of us.

As Leo Spitzer points out, all creatures share this one law of
sensual love because they are subject to the same law of world
harmony. [51] Love and harmony are essential features of the Chris-

---

(Ed. R. Sharrock [Oxford, 1960], p. 123). Here, then, the figure of the
shepherd is employed as a depository of spiritual truths. Shepherds are able
to perceive these truths better than other individuals because by living
closer to Nature they live closer to truth.

[50]
        Con mi llorar las piedras enternecen
        su natural dureza y la quebrantan;
        los árboles parece que s'inclinan;
        las aves que m'escuchan, quando cantan,
        con differente boz se condolecen
        y mi morir cantando m'adevinan;
           las fieras que reclinan
           su cuerpo fatigado
           dexan el sossegado
        sueño por escuchar mi llanto triste.

With my weeping the stones soften and break their natural hard-
ness; the trees seem to bend over; the birds, it seems, listen to
me, and when they sing they take pity in various cadences; and
singing, they sense my dying; the beasts which are resting their
tired bodies leave their peaceful dream to listen to my sad weeping.
See Garcilaso de la Vega, *Obras completas,* ed. Elias L. Rivers (Madrid,
1964), p. 75.

[51] Leo Spitzer, *Classical and Christian Ideas of World Harmony* (Baltimore, 1963), pp. 97-98. Spitzer also refers to the following examples of the
sensual harmony in Tasso's *La Gerusalemme liberata:*

tian Paradise. The atmosphere of sensual love and the sensual harmony which pervades the pastoral milieu of the Renaissance is an imperfect echo of the spiritual love and the divine harmony of Paradise.

It is such a pseudo-paradise which Sincero, the protagonist of *Arcadia*, enters. He confesses to his shepherd's pipe that he is not a shepherd, having been born in Naples:

> ... il quale ti compose di queste canne, quando in Arcadia venne, [venne] non come rustico pastore ma come coltissimo giovane, benche sconosciuto e peregrino di amore (p. 219).

> ... he who composed you out of these reeds, when he came to Arcadia, [came] not as a rustic shepherd but as a most refined youth, although unknown and a pilgrim of love.

Sincero is a victim of problematic love. Having failed to gain the attention of the beloved, he could not bear to be near her any more and left, wandering about aimlessly until he happened to arrive in Arcadia. Here in the realm of abundant nature he feels continuously reminded of his lady:

> Io non veggio nè monte, nè selva alcuna, che tuttavia non mi persuada di doverlavi ritrovare, quantunque a pensarlo mi paia impossibile. Niuna fiera, nè ucello, nè ramo vi sento movere, ch'io non mi gire paventoso per mirare si fusse essa in queste parti venuta ad intendere la misera vita. ch'io sostegno per lei: similmente niuna

---

> Vezzosi augelli infra le verdi fronde
> temprano a prova lascivette note;
> mormora l'aura, e fa le foglie e l'onde
> garrir, che variamente ella percote (XVI, 12).

The birds frolic among the green leaves, to make an early test of their lusty song. The breeze murmurs and makes the leaves and waves sway under the repeated impact:

> Tacque; e concorde de gli augelli il coro,
> quasi approvando, il canto indi ripiglia.
> Raddoppian le colombe i baci loro;
> ogni animal d'amar si riconsiglia (XVI, 16).

She fell silent; and as though approving, the choir of the birds renews its song. The doves multiply their kisses, and every animal takes to loving.

> altra cosa vedere vi posso, che prima non mi sia cagione
> di rimembrarmi con più fervore e sollicitudine di lei; e
> mi pare che le concave grotte, i fonti, le valli, i monti,
> con tutte le selve la chiamino, a gli altri arbusti risoneno
> sempre il nome di lei (p. 111).

> I do not see any mountain or forest which does not
> keep persuading me that I shall find her there, although
> on thinking about it, it seems to me impossible. Not one
> beast, or bird, or branch, do I see move that I do not turn
> around in fear to see if she might have come here to hear
> of the miserable life that I suffer for her hake. Similarly
> I cannot see any other object there which does not right
> away make me recall her with more fervor and anxiety.
> And it seems to me that the hollow grottoes, the fountains,
> the valleys, the mountains, and all the forests are echoing
> her name with the other bushes.

Sincero's experience is similar to Dante's: the association of the
lady with the respective paradise. Like the *peregrino* Dante,
Sincero is a *peregrino di amore* whose wandering ends in this
"paradise." Nevertheless Sincero's *peregrinatio* differs radically
from that of Dante. The latter confidently expects to see Beatrice
because he has been advised that he will. Thus his *peregrinatio*
to her shows a purposeful direction and he is aware that he is
making progress. Moreover, the same *peregrinatio* is also fulfilling
a Christian purpose, the ascent of the penitent soul straining for
the rewards of Paradise. Sincero, on the other hand, had no explicit intention of coming to *Arcadia*; he merely drifted into it.
At no time is he conscious of making progress towards reaching
his beloved; his *peregrinatio* consists of an aimless wandering in
absence of her. Also, unlike Paradise, the pagan Arcadia has no
spiritual rewards available to attract him.

Yet, once he has entered Arcadia, Sincero does experience some
of its benefits, for here he can give voice to his love problem in
the presence of sympathetic listeners, thereby obtaining relief.
In the normal everyday world Sincero would have found it difficult
to encounter such sympathy. Society inhibits the exclusive dedication to love, whereas the pastoral milieu encourages it. Even if
the Arcadia which he encounters is only a pale reflection of the
primeval Golden Age paradise, there exists at least a nostalgic

desire for that blissful age, a desire to find the environment most
conducive for the practice of love. The pastoral environment
comes closest to fulfilling this desire, because it most resembles
the Golden Age condition. Even though it is an imperfect copy, the
pastoral milieu by its very nature contributes to the attempted
reconstruction of the Golden Age by encouraging the practice of
love. As Bembo asserts, the practice of love in itself may conjure
up that happy age:

> Amor, la tua virtute
> non è dal mondo e da la gente intesa,
> che, da viltate offesa,
> segue suo danno e fuggo sua salute.
> Ma se fosser tra noi ben conosciute
> l'opre tue, come là dove risplende
> più del tuo raggio puro,
> camin dritto e securo
> prenderia vostra vita, che no 'l prende
> e tornerian con la prima beltade
> gli anni de l'oro e la felice etade. [52]

Love, your advantages are not understood by the world
and its people, who, outraged by meanness, pursue their
affliction and avoid their relief. But if your works were
as well known among us as up there, where your beams
shine brighter, our life would take a straight and safe
course — which it does not do now — and the Golden
Age with its pristine beauty and happy time would return.

Love, then, can recall the Golden Age, and vice versa. Since
society is alien to both love and the Golden Age, it can bring
about neither of the two conditions. If, therefore, an individual
sought the experience of true love, he would need to enter an
environment which encompassed at least part of these two conditions. The pastoral milieu of Renaissance fiction fulfilled this
demand in the realm of imagination. It is in this sense that the
pastoral romance represents the imaginary solution to a latent
psychic need of a society which was able to envision ideal love
but found it impossible to realize that ideal in its midst. In the
same manner in which Sincero embarked upon a *peregrinatio* to

---

[52] Pietro Bembo, *Degli Asolani*, in *Prose e Rime*, p. 320.

escape unsympathetic society, and to find solace in Arcadia, the reader of the pastoral novel could estrange himself temporarily from his own reality and immerse himself in the contemplation of a more perfect world of love. Symptomatic of this desire to escape is the habit of writers of attributing to shepherds the identity of real people. To place a friend in Arcadia was a gesture of homage because it meant the bestowal of a highly desired though imaginary bliss.

The nature and circumstances of Sincero's arrival in Arcadia thus serves to elucidate the attitude of an age. His case is matched by a parallel one in Gil Polo's novel *La Diana enamorada* (1564). Here Marcelio and Alcida are about to be married, but they become separated on their way to the wedding through a combination of accidents and treachery. Marcelio sets out in search of his beloved, wandering on a "peregrinación" [53] through the countryside. He is engaged in a *peregrinatio* of love, a temporary wandering in absence from the beloved, which also occurs in the Byzantine romance. However, the lovers do not meet in their home town but on the pastoral scene which they both entered in pastoral disguise. Here both meet with the sympathy of the fellow *pastores* and are finally reconciled by the *sabia* Felicia, who also performs the marriage ceremony. Seen from their own viewpoint, of course, their arrival here seemed haphazard. However, nowhere else than on the pastoral milieu would they have met with such profound understanding of their problems, an understanding which expedited the process of their reconciliation. For them the pastoral world was thus a necessary destination of their *peregrinatio*. [54]

---

[53] Gil Polo, *La Diana enamorada*, p. 142.

[54] That is, the lovers achieve their union in the Arcadian pastoral world. A similar association between the desire for union and the Golden Age is echoed in Calderón's play *La vida es sueño*. Here Rosaura disguises herself with the pseudonym of Astrea. Astrea is the goddess of justice and also the patroness of the Golden Age as Virgil testified in Ecloga IV, v. 6:

iam redit Virgo, redeunt Saturnia regnia.

Now the virgin [Astrea] returns, and the reign of Saturn [presiding over the Golden Age] returns.

Lope de Vega also certifies it in *El peregrino en su patria* (pp. 428-429):

Guerras el mundo afligían
por la mar y por la tierra

If the pastoral world marked the logical termination of a lover's *peregrinatio,* [55] then inversely an absence from it could likewise be a *peregrinatio,* as exemplified by the pastoral trilogy of Francisco Rodrigues Lobo. In Part II, entitled *O pastor peregrino* (1608), Lereno, a shepherd exiled from his paradise-like homeland, recalls the vicissitudes of his life:

> Fuy jà Pastor, & agora peregrino
> Com o cuydado, & trajo differente
> Vou tras de minha morte, ou meu destino.
> Fuy livre em outro estado, & fuy contente,
> Amor me fez cativo de hum cuydado,
> E eu me entreguey cativo livremente.
> Tive amigos, cabana, & tive gado,
> Tive descanso, & foy de pouca dura,
> Que nunca dura muyto hum doce estado. [56]

> que faltaban de aquel siglo
> la paz y la bella Astrea.

Wars afflicted the earth on sea and on land, because peace and the beautiful Astrea [who ruled the earth during] that [Golden] Age, were absent.

By adopting this name Rosaura associates the condition of the Golden Age with the restoration of her pristine honor and perhaps even the love of her former lover Astolfo. Moreover she is characterized by Clotaldo as a *peregrina:*

> Extranjeros peregrinos,
> libres estáis (I, 8).

Wandering strangers, you are free.

For Rosaura, then, the striving for the return of her honor and love is symbolized by the metaphor of a *peregrinatio amoris* to a paradisiacal condition.

[55] This process is also evident in Góngora's *Las soledades* (1613). The protagonist described as *el peregrino* suffers from unrequited love. In despair he has taken to sea and, shipwrecked, arrives in the idyllic surroundings where he finds a degree of distraction if not consolation. This flight away from the place of unhappiness to solitude or semisolitude of nature is a recurring motif in Spanish literature, as Karl Vossler has demonstrated in his book *La poesía de la soledad en España* (Buenos Aires, 1946).

[56] Francisco Rodrigues Lobo, *Corte na aldea* & *obras pastoras* (Lisboa, 1722), p. 26. Leriano's companion Oriano is likewise a *peregrino* for reasons of love:

> Este habito vesti de peregrino
> Por não ver de meu bem, triste, apartida
> E vou chorando agora de contino
> A gloria por meus erros mal perdida (p. 191).

I was once a shepherd and am now a wanderer.
[Burdened] with trouble and [dressed in] a different suit
I go toward my death or my destiny.

Once under different circumstances I was unburdened
and happy, then Love imprisoned me with trouble, and I
freely surrendered into captivity.

I had friends, a hut and a herd; I had rest; but it did
not last long, for a pleasant condition does not last long.

For him the absence from home also means absence from his
beloved; he too, then, is embarked on a *peregrinatio* of love, a
wandering in absence. In the company of another fellow-*peregrino*,
Oriano, he roves through pastoral and non-pastoral surroundings,
allowing himself to be borne along by the whim of fortune. However, he is never restored to his erstwhile happiness. In the
concluding part of the trilogy, entitled *O Desenganado* (1614), he
withdraws with his hopes dashed in order to live the life of a
hermit and reflect on the *engano* of his life while at the same
time preparing more intensely for the afterlife.

This note of irrevocable loss of the happiness of the native
"paradise" appears even more intensely in Lope de Vega's *Arcadia*
(1598). Here the shepherd Anfriso loves Belisarda; but through the
intrigues of malevolent shepherds he is exiled and is "de pastor
hecho peregrino." Circumstances, however, permit him to return:

Anfriso . . . , enternecido del amor de la patria y del ma-
terno . . . , desde el famoso puerto donde estaba volvió a
la patria, a la cual después de larga peregrinación y sucesos llegó. . . ." [57]

His exile is a *peregrinatio*, and since absence form Arcadia also
means absence from Belisarda, it is a *peregrinatio* of love. Yet,
the desired return does not afford him the happiness which he
expected. Suspicions of jealousy arise between the lovers, and out

---

I dressed in this pilgrim's habit, sadly unable to see my dear
[beloved], and now I weep continuously for the glory lost through
my blunders.

Oriano is not a shepherd; like Sincero he comes from outside the pastoral
world, and his *peregrinatio* too takes him to that place. Unlike Sincero,
however, he eventually regains his love and returns home again.

[57] Lope de Vega, *Arcadia*, BAE, XXXVIII, 91a.

of mutual spite each seeks a love affair with an outsider; Belisarda even marries an unloved shepherd. In the final parting scene they bewail in unison the potential common happiness which they lost because of their morbid suspicions. [58]

Profoundly disenchanted with the results of his love affair, Anfriso undertakes a *peregrinación* to the *templo del desengaño,* in order to gain the wisdom which would enable him to recognize his previous errors. His guide Polinesta duly enlightens him:

> Amor es ocio, ningún ocupado amó, ningún ocioso dejó de errar. Los daños de la ociosidad ¿a quién no son notorios? (p. 122).

> Love is idleness; no one who has ever been occupied ever loved; no idler ever avoided straying. Who is not aware of the ill effects of idleness?

Polinesta's judgment on love is severe, but not without justification. The pastoral world is the epitome of idleness. The shepherds accomplish nothing outside of their devoted pursuit of love. In the case of Anfriso this pursuit leads to nothing. Of his past life nothing remains but the bitterness of the *desengaño.* Now one of the outstanding features of the Counter Reformation was its insistence that life should not be wasted in idle pursuits but dedicated as much as possible to spiritual enlightenment. [59] It fostered thereby a habit of thought which consisted in looking at life as a whole and examining it in perspective even when one is engaged in pursuits of limited scope. Accordingly, an action should be performed with an awareness of its import for spiritual life as a whole. Correspondingly, as we noted earlier, the *peregrinatio* of love, more often than not, called to mind the wider scope

---

[58] Anfriso starts a relationship with Anarda. She knows that she has a rival; yet after he parts with Belisarda she is nevertheless ready to accept him again,

> ausente mío, peregrino de mi alma y estranjero de mi vida. ... ¿Cómo has estado sin mí? (p. 106b).

> My absent [darling], pilgrim of my soul and stranger of my life, how could you bear being without me?

She too regards his absence from her as a *peregrinatio.*

[59] Lope, plainly though appropriately, states that Anfriso, after terminating his love affair, has "retirado a mejor vida" (p. 121a).

of the *peregrinatio* of life. Life as depicted in the pastoral novel was almost exclusively dedicated to the quest of the incidental, worldly love so that it omitted the thought of life's purpose. Through the experience of the *desengaño* Anfriso realizes this deficiency and attempts to atone for it.

The case of Anfriso thus demonstrates the profound problem which surrounded the application of the concept of *peregrinatio* to human love. In the Christian sense *peregrinatio* is primarily a spiritual term, implying renunciation, devotion. The troubadours then initiated the imitation of the spiritual *peregrinatio* and its application to human love; and in time the whole interior logic of that religious concept was secularized. Hardships, renunciation, and devotion undertaken for the sake of human love became desirable. And just as the spiritual *peregrinatio* had its end-point in the Heavenly Paradise, so its humanized counterpart, the *peregrinatio amoris,* acquired its own version of paradise, whose ultimate manifestation was the pastoral milieu of Renaissance fiction. The close parallel which existed between the spiritual and the humanized *peregrinatio* is evidenced by the fact that both frequently occurred together within the same work.

Nevertheless Christian thought never quite acquiesced in this application of spiritual terms for human love. The concept of *peregrinatio* implied a spiritual exertion and devotion which was suitable only for a goal which was as lasting as eternal life. The same exertion when applied to transient human objectives implied a misplaced effort. [60] The commitment to transient goals was

---

[60] The difference between the erotic and the spiritual *peregrinationes* is very apparent in Fray Bartolomé Ponce's interesting account of how he conceived the idea of writing a divinized version of Jorge de Montemayor's *Diana,* which he would call *Clara Diana a lo divino:*

> In the year 1559 I was at the court of our lord King Phillip II, on business in behalf of my monastery of Santa Fe, and I associated with the courtly gentlemen. There I saw and read the *Diana* of Jorge de Montemayor, which was as well received as any other book in Spanish that I had ever seen. I had a great desire to become acquainted with its author. That was readily arranged for me, for within ten days we were both opportunely invited by an illustrious gentleman who was extremely fond of verse, and poetry in general. This subject then came up in an after-dinner conversation. Happy and eager I began to tell him [i.e., Montemayor] how much I had looked forward to his presence and his friend-

bound to result in profound disillusionment, all the more so, the greater the previous commitment had been. Thus when Europe in the sixteenth century experienced the spiritual revival which was marked by the Reformation and the Counter Reformation the tendency arose of reemphasizing the spiritual significance of *peregrinatio*. This revival will be the subject of our next chapter.

---

ship, if only to take courage to tell him how much he was wasting his delicate mind on the superfluous potentials of the soul in thinking up conceits, making rhymes, fabricating stories, and composing books about worldly love in secular style. He replied with a composed smile: 'Father Ponce, let the friars perform penitence for all others; as for us noblemen, our profession consists of the [pursuit of] arms and love.' 'I promise you, Señor Montemayor,' I said, 'to compose with my rough and crude ability another *Diana,* which shall pursue yours with crude hammerblows.' With this, and much laughter, the gathering ended and we took leave. May God pardon his soul, for I never saw him again. A few months later they told me that a good friend of his had killed him out of some jealousy or love affair. [This demonstrates the] most just verdict of God, for it punishes a man most where he is implicated the most. See him now, he lived by love and grew up with it; he became entangled in love and always contemplated it; he exalted love, wrote about love, and died for love.

Translated from M. Menéndez Pelayo, *Orígenes de la novela* (Buenos Aires, 1943), IV, 130-131.

Chapter III

THE PILGRIMAGE OF LIFE

The Concept of Peregrinatio Vitae *in the Baroque*

We noted in the preceding chapters that the various types of *peregrinationes* were frequently linked with the concept of *peregrinatio vitae,* a metaphor which circumscribes man's exile from Paradise and his unstable, wandering sojourn on earth. We also noted that this association was strongest in those works which stressed a profoundly Christian outlook on the world. After the Council of Trent (1545-1563) the Christianizing appeal of art became not only emphatic but obligatory. According to the art theory of the Counter Reformation, art should not merely entertain but instruct as well, educate the audience in the principles of Christian faith. Among these principles the Biblical notion that life on earth is a *peregrinatio* was a central one. The task of a writer who wished to adopt this notion for his work would consist in exploiting it in all its consequences, in dramatizing it in order to intensify the reader's consciousness of it.

In Spain the notion of *peregrinatio vitae* was especially prevalent, as Antonio Vilanova has demonstrated. [1] Surveying the literature of the Spanish baroque, he concludes that

> in the Spanish novel of the sixteenth and seventeenth centuries there exists a fictional character which must be

---

[1] Translated from "El peregrino andante en el *Persiles* de Cervantes," *Boletín de la Real Academia de buenas letras de Barcelona,* XXI (1949), 97-159.

clearly differentiated from the knight errant, the *pícaro* and the shepherd and which must be designated with the term *peregrino*.[2]

This *peregrino andante*, best personified in the figure of Persiles in Cervantes' work *Persiles y Sigismunda*, represents in his view "the perfect ideal of the Christian gentleman of the Counter Reformation" (148). The *peregrino andante* possesses the virtues of the knight-courtier which Erasmus outlined in the *Enchiridion*. At the same time the *peregrino* supersedes the figure of the knight in that he is no longer concerned with heroic exploits. Instead, he devotes himself to a peripatetic experience of the world in a manner similar to that of the *pícaro*.[3] In doing so he becomes a symbol of man performing his *peregrinatio* on earth:

> The *peregrino* is the symbol of Christian man, a descendant of the Biblical idea of the earthly pilgrimage, which considers man as a pilgrim, exile, and stranger on earth (158).

The Biblical Origin of PEREGRINATIO VITAE

Vilanova quite accurately traces the origin of the *peregrino andante* of the baroque directly to the Biblical metaphor of *peregrinatio vitae*. Nevertheless, it is important to bear in mind that the Bible preceded the baroque period by a millennium and a half. In the course of this time the metaphor produced derivative meanings which differed from, yet coexisted with, the original meaning. The baroque concept of *peregrinatio vitae* may thus be said to derive from two sources. First, it is taken directly from the Bible; and second, it results from a long historical evolution which proceeded independently of the Biblical meaning. To

---

[2] Vilanova, *Peregrino,* p. 158.

[3]   As a spiritualized and humanized knight-errant, the *peregrino* with his characteristic scorn for fame takes the place of the elaborate pride of the chivalric ideal. Thus he counteracts the pure fantasy with which the chivalric novel presents the superhuman destiny of the hero with the idealized reality which symbolizes man's human condition.
Vilanova, p. 150.

analyze the two sources and their combined effect on baroque literature will be the purpose of this chapter.

Biblical references to the *peregrinatio vitae* are as numerous as they are various in their application. In what follows I shall cite only a few quotations which Vilanova considers as most characteristic of the Spanish baroque. In one instance Jacob tells Pharaoh his age:

> Quot sunt dies vitae tuae? Respondit: Dies peregrinationis meae centum triginta annorum sunt, parvi et mali, et non pervenerunt usque ad dies patrum meorum quibus peregrinati sunt (Gen. 47, 8-9).

> [And Pharaoh said unto Jacob,] How old art thou? [And Jacob] said [unto Pharaoh]: The days of the years of my pilgrimage are an hundred and thirty years; few and evil have the days of the years of my life been, and have not attained unto the days of the years of the life of my fathers in the days of their pilgrimage.

Here *peregrinatio* designates a life span. In the next quotation from Ecclesiastes *peregrinatio* signifies a particular kind of life, a life full of hardships:

> Quid necesse est hominis maiora se quaerere,
> Cum ignoret quid conducat sibi in vita suae
> Numero dierum peregrinationis suae
> Et tempore quod velut umbra praeterit? (Eccl. 7, 1)

> For who knoweth what is good for man in this life, all the days of his vain life which he spendeth as a shadow? for who can tell a man what shall be after him under the sun?

It appears, however, that the sense of *peregrinatio* as a life full of hardship is not limited to Biblical usage, because we also find it in a pagan grave inscription of antiquity:

> Multis annis navigando et peregrinando hanc sede peti. [4]

---

[4] Quoted from Richard Lattimore, *Themes in Greek and Latin Epitaphs,* in *Illinois Studies in Language and Literature,* XXVIII (Urbana, 1942), 167.

Here the deceased sees the grave as a resting place after toilsome years of instability and wandering. This resting place is, of course, a rather untranscendental one; it is merely an earthly depository for the body. Similarly the idea of *peregrinatio* has no transcendental significance here. It refers only to the earthly life; its frame of reference is limited to the earthly sphere. A Christian would object to this frame of reference as being insufficient. His religion, after all, teaches him to look beyond the grave, and into eternity. And seen from the perspective of eternity, a lifetime occupies only a brief span. It is only a temporary sojourn away from the true home of Paradise from where he was exiled through original sin. The Christian, then, would feel the implication of the concept of *peregrinatio vitae* with a special intensity, simply because he had something better to look forward to. He would tend to be consumed by the incessant longing to abandon his earthly dwelling place in favor of the Heavenly one. St. Paul exemplifies this state of mind very accurately:

> Audentes igitur semper scientes, quoniam, dum sumus in corpore, peregrinamur a Domino (per fidem enim ambulamus, et non per speciem), audemus autem et bonam voluntatem habemus magis peregrinari a corpore et praesentes esse ad Dominum. Et ideo contendimus sive ausentes sive praesentes placere illi (2. Cor. 5, 6-9).

> Therefore we are always confident, knowing that, whilst we are at home in the body, we are absent from the Lord: (For we walk by faith, not by sight:) We are confident, I say, and willing rather to be absent from the body, and to be present with the Lord. Wherefore we labour, that whether present or absent, we may be accepted of him.

St. Paul's reaction to the *peregrinatio vitae* is very explicit: he deplores it. Rather than be absent from God he would prefer to be absent from his body and to be near God. This is not possible, however, until after death when the soul may separate from the body and ascend towards God. As long as one is alive, however, one may wish for such a union.

For St. Paul, then, the *peregrinatio vitae* is a disagreeable condition, which he would gladly overcome in any way he could. This reaction is also apparent in the *Confessions* of St. Augustine, who likewise laments the great distance which separates him from God, a distance which had been even greater before his conversion, because of his involvement in sin:

> Vbi ergo mihi eras et quam longe? et longe peregrinabar abs te. ... [5]

> Where were you then [Lord] and how far away? For I strayed far from you. ...

This painful absence, he hopes, may end with the return to Paradise which he and his fellow citizens here on earth so strongly desire:

> Meminerint cum affectu pio parentum meorum in hac luce transitoria, et fratrum meorum sub te patre in matre Catholica, et civium meorum in aeterna Jerusalem, cui suspirat peregrinatio populi tui ab exitu usque ad reditum (IX, 13).

> May [the readers of my *Confessions*] with pious affection remember my parents in this transitory light [of day], along with my brothers who are contained in the Catholic Mother Church under [the auspices of] You, the Father, as well as those who are to be my fellow-citizens in that eternal Jerusalem, for which your people in exile yearn so much from their birth until their return.

For St. Augustine this absence from God has in addition a very personal significance: it poses for him a dilemma which affects the task of writing his confession, namely the problem of self-knowledge. The following passage illustrates this concern:

> Tu enim, domine, dijudicas me, quia etsi nemo scit hominum, quae sunt hominis, nisi spiritus hominis, qui in ipso est, tamen est aliquid hominis, quod nec ipse scit spiritus hominis, qui in ipso est, tu autem, Domine, scis ejus omnia, qui fecisti eum. Ego vero quamvis prae tuo conspectu me despiciam, et aestimem me terram et cinerem, tamen aliquid de te scio, quod de me nescio. Et certe videmus nunc per speculum in aenigmate, nondum facie

---

[5] St. Augustine, *Confessionum Libri* XIII, *PL* XXXII, Bk. III, Ch. 6.

ad faciem: et ideo, quamdiu peregrinor abs te, mihi sum praesentior quam tibi, et tamen te novi nullo modo posse violari; ego vero quibus temptationibus resistere valeam, quibusve non valeam, nescio. Et spes est, quia fidelis es, qui nos non sinis tentari supra quam possumus ferre, sed facis cum tentatione etiam exitum ut possimus sustinere. Confitear ergo quid de me sciam, confitear et quid de me nesciam. Quoniam et quod de me scio, te mihi lucente scio; et quod de me nescio, tamdiu nescio, donec fiant tenebrae meae sicut meridies in vultu tuo (X, 5).

You, Lord, are judging me, because no one knows the ways of man, but the spirit that is within him. Yet there are some aspects of man which even his spirit within him does not know. But You, Lord, Who have made him, know everything about him. As for me, although I despise myself in Your sight and think of myself as mere dust and ashes, I do know something about You which I do not know about myself. For surely, now we see through a glass darkly, and not yet face to face. Therefore, as long as I am absent from You, I am closer to me than to You. Yet I know of no way that You can be violated, while I do not know which temptations I am able to resist and which not. But there is hope, because You are faithful and will not allow us to be tempted above our ability to bear it. I will therefore confess what I know about myself as well as what I do not know. For, if You enlighten me I will come to know even what I do know about myself. And what I do not know of myself I shall not know until my darkness becomes as light as the noonday in your sight.

St. Augustine's primary purpose in writing his *Confessions* was to present a report of his conversion, with the changes in spiritual state which it involved. Yet no man can pretend to know his spiritual state perfectly; for as long as man lives in his earthly *peregrinatio*, distant from God, he remains handicapped, because his senses are inadequate instruments of cognition. [6] His perspective is dulled; everything appears to him as if through a glass

---

[6] St. Augustine's obsessive concern for the need of knowledge of self as well as of God finds its stylistic reflection in the repetitiveness within the following phrase: "Cognoscam te, cognitor meus, cognoscam, sicut et cognitus sum" (X, 1).

darkly. In order to know himself, therefore, man needs the help of God, who created him, programmed him, so to speak, infused him with the spiritual ingredients which he, God, knows best. To God St. Augustine will confess everything, not only those things which he comprehends, but also those things which baffle him, hoping that God will, by a ray of inspiration, enlighten him about their significance.

Peregrinatio Vitae *Applied: The Rise of Asceticism*

For St. Augustine, then, the condition of *peregrinatio vitae* was doubly disagreeable; however, it had unwillingly to be endured until life's end. For Christians in general it was also an abnormal condition. Not only was the *peregrinatio* a punishment, an exile from Paradise, but it was a punishment for a sin which was perpetrated not by the individual but by mankind's distant ancestor. Worse yet, there seemed to be little which the individual could do to atone for this inherited guilt and to reduce his extended prison term on earth. Such an acute paradox was bound to put considerable stress on the conscience of the individual, a stress to which sensitive minds quite naturally reacted. At length a solution was found, and it was found by the men who became the Egyptian desert monks. In the following passage St. Chrysostom comments on them:

> Εἶδες ἡδίκα ἡμᾶς ὤνησαν οἱ ξένοι καὶ παρεπίδεμοι οὗτοι, οἱ τῆς ἐρήμου πολῖται. μάλλον δὲ οἱ τῶν οὐρανῶν πολῖται; Ἡμεῖς γαρ τῶν οὐρανῶν ξένοι, πολῖται δὲ τῆς γῆς. οὗτοι δὲ τουναντίον.[7]

> Do you see how greatly these strangers and aliens have benefitted us, these citizens of the wilderness, or rather, these citizens of Heaven? We are strangers with respect to Heaven, and citizens of this earth. With these it is otherwise.

Most of us, St. Chrysostom notes, feel greater attachment to the world than to Heaven. But the desert hermits have forsaken

---

[7] "In Mattheum Homilia," *PG*, LVIII, col. 548. St. Chrysostom employs the Biblical word ξένος which in the Vulgate is occasionally translated as *peregrinus*. See e.g., Hebr. 11, 13.

the normal way of life in this world and live as voluntary exiles from it in order to merit the happiness of Heaven. These ξένοι have, in effect, become citizens of Heaven (τῶν οὐρανῶν πολῖται) by becoming citizens of the wilderness (τῶν ἐρήμου πολῖται). These monks, therefore, constitute living examples of the Biblical theme; they are illustrations of the ξενιτεία, the *peregrinatio*. [8] However, to live as a ξένος it was not absolutely necessary to turn one's back to the world and escape into the desert. It sufficed, especially in later times, to live in a monastic cell and to observe the rules of silence. [9] One could, in fact, live as a ξένος in the midst of the tumultuous world simply by cutting oneself off from it by refusing to communicate with other people and by shunning all the normal rituals of human association. [10]

Whether he exiled himself geographically or psychologically, the ξένος, the embodiment of the Biblical *peregrinatio vitae,* was in effect the forerunner of the monk. Eventually the ideal of monasticism spread westward and it did so within the framework of the concept of *peregrinatio*. Irish monks in particular were

---

[8] ξενιτεία becomes almost a technical term to describe a condition indispensable to the life of a monk:

Ἔλεγεν ὁ ἀββᾶς Ἀνδρέας. Πρεπει τῷ μοναχῷ τα τρία ταυτα. ἡ ξενιτεία, ἡ πτωχεία, καὶ ἡ σιωπὴ ἐν ὑπομονῇ.

The abbot Andreas used to say: Three things above all are appropriate for the monk: *peregrinatio*, poverty, and silence in patience.

See *Apophthegmata Patrum, PG*, LXV, 136:

[9] Ἡρώτησεν ὁ ἀββᾶς Λογγῖνος τὸν ἀββᾶν Λούχιόν, ποτε τρεῖς λογισμοὺ, λέγων. Θέλω ξενιτεῦσαι. Λέγει αὐτῷ ὁ γέρων. Ἐάν μὴ κρατήσῃς τῆς γλώσσες σου, οὐκ εἰ ξένος ὅπου εαν ἀπελτες. Καὶ ὦδε οὖν κράτησον τῆς γλώσσες σου, χαὶ ξένος εἰ.

The abbot Longinus asked the abbot Lucius about three thoughts: "I wish to live in a state of *peregrinatio*." The old man said to this: "If you do not master your tongue, you will not be a *peregrinus,* wherever you may go. Therefore master your tonge, and you will be a *peregrinus!*"

See *Apophthegmata, PG*, LXV, 256.

[10] Πάλιν ἕτερος ἐξ ἡμῶν εἶπεν αὐτῷ. Τί ἐστι ξενιτεία, πατερ; χαι εἶπε. Οὐκ ἔχω πρᾶγμα, ἐν παντί τόπω ὅπου ἐὰν απερχῃ. χαὶ αὕτη εστὶν ἡ ξενιτεία.

Once again one of us said: "What is a *peregrinatio?* And he said: "Be silent, and at every place say, 'This does not concern me'; that is *peregrinatio*."

See *Apophthegmata, PG*, LXV, 373.

eager to imitate the lives of the Egyptian desert fathers. As a result a considerable number of these monks left their homeland to live abroad as strangers. They labelled this action as *peregrinari pro Christo* and modelled it on the *peregrinatio* of Abraham. [11] Some of these monks put to sea and set out to live on the small barren islands which surround the British Isles. Thus on his sea voyage St. Brendan meets such hermits — they are called in Anglo-Norman *pelerins* — on the Island of Ailbee. [12] Other monks went to the continent to live out the concept of *peregrinatio* either by performing difficult missionary work or by establishing monasteries. [13] Medieval treatises, therefore, frequently refer to these and other monks as *peregrini*. [14]

Later ages, too, retained this concept. In the following sonnet published in 1617, Alonso de Bonilla uses it to eulogize the monastic life of Santa Teresa and her followers:

> Los preceptos de Cristo son caminos
> Que van a dar a la ciudad segura,
> Aunque algún polvo en su cristiana anchura
> Cobran de imperfección los peregrinos.
>
> Mas los consejos altos y divinos
> De estrecha religión y de clausura
> Son sendas por do puede el alma pura
> Ir como por espejos cristalinos.
>
> Por éstas pués Teresa y su grey santa
> Con pies descalzos van ganando prendas,
> De que su amor en Dios los eterniza;

---

[11] Dom Louis Gougaud, *Gaelic Pioneers of Christianity*, trans. Victor Collins (Dublin, 1923), pp. 6-7.

[12] St. Ailbee himself is called a *pelerin* by his surviving disciples who continue to live on the island:

> Uitante anz ad que prist sa fin
> A saint Albeu le pelerin.

It has been twenty years since St. Ailbee, the pilgrim, found his end.

Quoted from *The Anglo Norman Voyage of St. Brendan*, ll. 721-722.

[13] Joseph P. Fuhrmann, *Irish Medieval Monasteries on the Continent* (Washington, 1927). See esp. pp. 1-13.

[14] See du Cange, *Glossarium Mediae et Infimae Latinitatis*, s.v. *peregrinatio*. One of the examples given here reports the meeting of an abbot with his "pilgrim monks *(cum Peregrinis monachis suis)*." For more information on this subject see also Jean Leclercq, "Monachisme et pérégrination du IXe au XIIe siècle," *Studia Monastica*, III (1961), 33-52.

Donde caminan con pureza tanta
Que no cogen más polvo en estas sendas
Que contemplar que son polvo y ceniza. [15]

The precepts of Christ are paths which will lead to the
secure city, even though the pilgrims will contract some
dust of imperfection in [the paths'] Christian narrowness.

But the lofty and Divine precepts of narrow religion
and confinement are paths by which the purified soul can
go as by crystalline mirrors.

By walking along these [paths], then, Teresa and her
saintly flock will, with their bare feet, earn rewards
whereby their love will eternalize them in God.

Where they will walk with such purity that they
will catch no more dust in these paths other than the
recognition that they are dust and ashes.

Bonilla characterizes those who follow the path of Christ's precepts
as *peregrinos* who will ultimately reach the merited Paradise.
Naturally, the prospect of following Christ is open to all Christians.
Monks or nuns, however, are different from ordinary Christians. For the average Christian walks a path which is still
relatively wide ("cristiana anchura") and he cannot totally escape
the dust which the morally corruptive, disintegrating world spreads
on him. For Teresa and her nuns, however, the path has narrowed
("estrecha religión") and the dust that reaches them is minimal.
By narrowing their path they have restricted their worldly concern
and detached themselves from it more than the ordinary Christian
could be expected to do. Because of this restriction and detachment
their pursuit of the *peregrinatio* has intensified. Whereas most
Christians live out the *peregrinatio vitae* passively, the monk or
nun does so actively. [16]

---

[15] *BAE*, XXXV, 44b.

[16] The *peregrinatio* of monasticism also serves as a motif in literature.
In Shakespeare's comedy *A Midsummer Night's Dream*, Theseus threatens
Hermia with the dreaded alternative of nunhood if she should refuse to marry
the man of his choice:

Therefore, fair Hermia, question your desires
Know of your youth, examine well your blood,
Whe'r, if you yield not to your father's choice,
You can endure the livery of a nun,

Monasticism, then, is the final result of the early Christian's intensified concern over the *peregrinatio vitae*. The pagan did not have this concern. He had after all nothing extraordinary to look forward to after death. He was convinced that he would descend into Hades, and, as Achilles testifies to Ulysses in *Odyssey* XI, afterlife is a rather tedious affair, not preferable to life itself. The Christian on the other hand was aware of the contrast which existed between the misery of his present life and the bliss of his real home in Paradise. He knew that the endpoint of the *peregrinatio vitae* was Paradise, and he wanted to insure his arrival there. Monasticism increased the chances that he would do so.

> For aye to be in shady cloister mew'd,
> To live a barren sister all your life,
> Chanting faint hymns to the cold fruitless moon.
> Thrice-blessed they that master so their blood,
> To undergo such maiden pilgrimage, ... (I, 1)

(Cited from *The Oxford Shakespeare*, p. 197a). We note that Theseus' view of nunhood is not without complexity. By characterizing the nuns as "thrice-blessed" he shows his ability to judge nunhood in a positive way. That is, for a tiny instant he views it, as did Bonilla, from the spiritual side. But unlike Bonilla he also regards it from the worldly side, as he betrays by the expressions "barren sister," "faint hymns," "cold fruitless moon." From the worldly point of view the cloistered pilgrimage of nunhood epitomizes the negation of vitality; it is something to be "endured." It is this view which predominates in Theseus, and which he communicates to his daughter.

Nunhood also appears as an alternative to married life in Mira de Amescua's play *El esclavo del demonio* (1612). Here Marcelo acknowledges with contentment that one of his two daughters has chosen the *peregrinatio* of nunhood:

> Tú, Leonor, que el pensamiento
> a Dios eterno ofreciste,
> en que yo vivo contento;
> ya que el estado elegiste,
> sabe elegir el convento.
> Tus intentos son divinos,
> que en esta vida en que estamos
> todos somos peregrinos
> del cielo, aunque caminamos
> por diferentes caminos.
> Cada estado, ya se sabe
> que es camino; cuál es grave,
> cuál es fácil; la casada
> lleva su cruz más pesada,
> y la monja menos grave.

The PEREGRINATIO *of Purgatorial Penitence*

The superseding of the pagan notion of the afterlife by the Christian one is perhaps the most effectively illustrated by Dante's *Divina Commedia*. In designing the Inferno, Dante draws on Vergil's *Aenid* VI where the souls of the virtuous as well as of the wicked are seen to share the same general underground dwelling. In the *Inferno*, likewise, the virtuous pagans remain underground, although they are allocated the preferred place of Limbo. On the other hand, the concept of the *Purgatorio* is entirely Christian. Like the Inferno, it too is occupied by sinners but these are redeemable and will eventually enter Paradise after a due period of penitence. As we noted earlier, Dante labels the penitents *peregrini.* [17] The trials and hardships of purgation therefore constitute a *peregrinatio,* whose purpose resembles that of the monastic *peregrinatio* in its striving for Paradise. Of course, the penitence of the monks takes place here on earth during their life time; it is a *peregrinatio vitae.* The penitence of purgatory,

---

> You, Leonor, who have chosen to offer your thoughts to the eternal God — of which I am happy — now that you have elected your station, select well your convent.
> Your intentions are Divine, for in this our life we are all strangers from Heaven, although we walk along different paths.
> Each station is well known to be a path; one is difficult, another is easy. The married woman carries her cross with greater burden, and the nun [carries it] less heavily.

(Cited from *Diez comedias del Siglo de Oro,* ed. Hymen Alpern and José Martel [New York, 1939], Act. 1, ll. 41-55.) Marcelo, unlike Theseus, regards nunhood from a purely spiritual point of view. He begins his analysis by stating that life is a *peregrinatio,* whose destination is Heaven. Of the different paths that lead to Heaven, monasticism constitutes one path, one type of peregrinatio. It is, in short, "a way of life." It is not, however, the only way. Marriage constitutes another path. Marriage therefore may itself be a *peregrinatio.* This is one view expressed by the French priest Simon Mars in his treatise *Mystère du voyage de Dieu:*

> Le mariage est un long pèlerinage ou sont trois ou quatre hotelleries: la première se nomme faux plaisire, la second repentir, la troisième misère; si vous passez plus avant, vous êtes en danger de trouver le désespoir.

> Marriage is a long pilgrimage, in which there are four inns. The first is called false pleasure, the second repentance, the third misery; if you go further, you risk finding despair.

Cited from Émile Littré, *Dictionnaire de la langue française,* s.v. *pèlerinage.*

[17] Dante, *Purgatorio,* II, 1. 63. See our Chapter I.

on the other hand, is more properly called a *peregrinatio mortis,* [18] because, with the exception of Dante, all the penitents are the souls of the dead. Nevertheless, there exists a close correlation between the two types of *peregrinationes* which we will illustrate with an analysis of the English morality play *Everyman.*

In this play Everyman is being surprised, in the midst of his worldly preoccupations, by a visit from Death, by whom he is instructed to prepare to die:

---

[18] The term *peregrinatio mortis* is a problematic one, because "life" and "death" are ambiguous notions in Christian thought. Nevertheless I have preferred it over the expression *peregrinatio aeternitatis,* because Purgatory does not yet participate in eternity in the full sense of the word. Eternity implies an absence of time, such as reigns in Paradise and Hell. In Purgatory, on the other hand, the earthly time notion is still in effect because the length of an individual's penitence is measured in years and centuries. Thus we may say that wherever and for as long as man finds himself in a state of *peregrinatio* he also faces the notion of time.

This close association of time with the idea of *peregrinatio* is explicitly stated in Shakespeare's tragedy *Richard II,* where Gaunt complains to Richard about his advancing age:

> Richard.   Why, uncle, thou hast many years to live.
> Gaunt.   But not a minute, king, that thou canst give:
>   Shorten my days thou canst with sullen sorrow,
>   And pluck nights from me, but not lend a morrow;
>   Thou canst help time to furrow me with age,
>   But stop no wrinkle in his pilgrimage;
>   Thy word is current with him for my death,
>   But dead, thy kingdom cannot buy my breath (I, 3).

Gaunt views the trail of advancing time like a pilgrimage. Like a pilgrim, time advances in sequences of steps, in segments of day and night. Each step, like each day or night, is a repetition of the previous one. We find a slight but unmistakable echo of this view of time or pilgrimage in the following statement by Macbeth:

> To-morrow, and to-morrow, and to-morrow,
> Creeps in this petty pace from day to day,
> To the last syllable of recorded time;
> And our yesterdays have lighted fools
> The way to dusty death (V, 5).

Macbeth too sees the passing of time as a series of segments of "tomorrow and tomorrow," segments which are repeated endlessly and monotonously like the repeated steps of the pilgrim. He exhibits thereby an extreme, oversensitive consciousness of time. This consciousness of time also accompanies the consciousness of the *peregrinatio vitae,* as Shakespeare's contemporary Samuel Purchas suggests:

> At sea ... only the Heaven and the inconstant shifting Elements which constantly put us in minde of our Pilgrimage, and how

> For I am commaunded a pilgrimage to take,
> and a great countes before God to make. [19]

Here the "pilgrimage" is not a *peregrinatio vitae* but a *peregrinatio mortis,* a journey to the other world which will take Everyman into the proximity of God. Since most men are sinners and must traverse Purgatory after death, Everyman, who by his very name represents a cross-section of mankind, will also go through it. The journey through Purgatory is therefore an integral part of his *peregrinatio mortis.*

Before he is to die, however, Everyman is allotted a brief time span during which he may prepare himself. Upon consulting Confession he receives this advice:

> I wyll you comfort / as well as I can
> And a precious iewell I wyll gyue the
> Called penaunce / voyder of aduersyte
> There with shall your bady chastysed be
> With abstinence stonge / that ye must endure
> Remember thy sauyour was scourged for the
> With sharpe scourges / and suffred it paciently
> So must thou / or thou passe thy pilgrimage
> Knowledge kepe hym on this vyage (ll. 556-566).

Confession urges Everyman to perform penance while he still has time. For if he fails to do so he will "passe," i.e., not accomplish his "pilgrimage." Here, then, "pilgrimage" refers to the

---

neare in a thin ship and thinner, weaker, tenderer body we dwell to death, teaching us daily to number our days, and apply our hearts to wisdome.

(*His Pilgrimes,* I, 56.) The *peregrinatio vitae* is a consequence of original sin; and it signifies man's continuing sinful condition on earth and time is its concomitant. The Christian term for the sinful world, *saeculum,* is therefore appropriately an expression of time. In Christian tradition, moreover, the age of the world is measured from the time of Adam's expulsion from Paradise. The notion of time thus arose when Adam initiated mankind's *peregrinatio.* Time then is a constant reminder of the sinful condition. And the greater the sin, the greater the consciousness of time. At the point where Macbeth makes his observation about time he is steeped in sin and guilt. We might conclude therefore the intensified awareness of time is, together with the heightened consciousness of the *peregrinatio vitae,* a characteristic of the spiritual revival of the baroque period.

[19] *Everyman,* ed. W. W. Greg (Vaduz, 1963), ll. 550-551.

ascetic penance performed during life, i.e., it is a *peregrinatio vitae*. By accomplishing it Everyman will attain a remission of his sins, thereby effecting a reduction of his purgatorial term:

> Nowe of penaunce I wyll wade the water clere
> To saue me fro purgatory that sharpe fyre (ll. 617-618).

In other words, Everyman may, by performing an ascetic *peregrinatio vitae*, reduce the length of his *peregrinatio mortis*, and mitigate its rigor. This constitutes an important recognition for Everyman, for now he knows that by taking proper action during the remainder of his life he may plan ahead for the future and to an extent also control it. And after the initial shock over the news of his imminent death, this recognition affords him a degree of comfort. For he realizes that, although death is inevitable, he does have an option: he may determine, if he chooses, the condition of his afterlife by performing a timely penitence.

Everyman's recognition also constitutes an important message for the audience, which is here witnessing the spectacle of death. The artistic presentation of the awareness of death preoccupied medieval writers profoundly, and it could take a variety of forms. One could, like François Villon, conjure up in poetic form the specter of death in its terrifying aspect of physical dissolution. Or one could view it with Christian resignation as a kindly agent of God, as did Jorge Manrique. In *Everyman* death is presented as a play, and it is "presented" in the real sense of the word. For most human beings regard death as a future event which is far too remote to arouse their concern. They prefer to concentrate their attention on the affairs of the present moment, because to the human mind the present is always more vivid than the abstract future. *Everyman* seeks to overcome, for a moment at least, this shortcoming of human awareness. By conjuring up dramatically the awareness of death, it makes the future event appear as a present one and impresses it on the minds of the audience with a terrifying sense of immediacy. It evokes the consciousness that death, although seemingly a future event, is in fact a constant potential presentness, which at any moment may turn into an actual fact. Most people are, after all, not aware of their own death until they feel its presence face to face. The devout Christian therefore should always regard death as imminent and maintain a constant state of preparedness.

The Devotional Pilgrimage

Everyman prepares himself with an ascetic *peregrinatio vitae*, whereby he may reduce his purgatorial term. People such as monks live all of their life in a state of *peregrinatio*, and they are, by this token, eligible to forego Purgatory and enter Paradise directly. But monks are professional *peregrini*, whereas Everyman is not. His *peregrinatio* encompasses only a very limited, though very decisive, time of his life; it is the *peregrinatio* of the layman. The layman thus has as much of a chance to work for his salvation as the professional monk, and he can accomplish his penitence in several ways. On the one hand, he can like Everyman mortify his body through self-flagellation. Or he can undertake a pilgrimage to the shrine of a saint, like the pilgrims in the *Canterbury Tales*:

> Commune penaunce is that preestes enioinen men comunly in certeyn caas; as for to goon, peradventure, naked in pilgrimages, or bare-foot. [20]

As the parson certifies, the performance of the pilgrimage is a means of reducing the pains of Purgatory and of expediting the soul on its progress to Paradise:

> I wol you telle a mery tale in prose
> To knytte up al this feeste, and made an ende.
> And Iesu, for his grace, wit me sende
> To shewe yow the wey, in this viage,
> Of thilke parfit glorious pilgrymage
> That highte Ierusalem celestial. [21]

The pilgrimage thus has the same effect as the ascetic *peregrinatio*. The latter, as we have seen, is an activated form of the originally passive *peregrinatio vitae* of the Bible, and it was directly derived from it. Whether the concept of the pilgrimage,

---

[20] Cited from "The Persones Tale," *The Complete Works of Geoffrey Chaucer*, ed. W. W. Skeat (Oxford, 1940), IV, 572.
[21] "The Parson's Prolog," *Works*, IV, 568.

too, stems from a direct application of the Biblical metaphor, I have been unable to determine. At any rate, Christian tradition did eventually associate the one with the other. This feature is perhaps most effectively illustrated in an *auto sacramental* by Calderón, *El año santo de Roma* (1650).

In this play Calderón celebrates the occasion of the Holy Year 1650 during which pilgrims to Rome could obtain special indulgences. The play does not, however, dramatize the historical event itself; rather it uses it only as a point of departure. For the *auto* is above all a dramatic representation of a Christian theme. [22] As a result the focus of the *auto* passes beyond the exteriors of the historical event and centers instead on the spiritual idea that lurks behind it. Thus the *auto* reflects the event as an x-ray picture reflects an object: it does not show the external contours but instead reveals the logic of an internal pattern, a spiritual logic. Accordingly in *El año santo de Roma* the pilgrimage to Rome is not represented as such, but in the form of the spiritual pattern which it embodies, namely the ascetic, penitential *peregrinatio* which it represents. Thus, whereas we should see the doors of St. Peter's cathedral opened to the pilgrims, we see instead the gates of Heaven opened to receive El Hombre, 'Everyman,' who is a *peregrinus* on earth:

> Venid, venid peregrinos
> venid, venid que este año
> la Puerta se abre que estuvo cerrada
> por tantas edades, por siglos tan largos;
> y pues que la Vida es jornada de todos
> dichosos aquellos que peregrinando
> merecen que el año reparta con ellos
> la acción de piadoso, el renombre de Santo. [23]

---

[22] Calderón states this concept of the *auto sacramental* in the Loa to *La segunda esposa.* In his view *autos* are

> sermones
> puestos en verso, en idea
> representable, cuestiones
> de la Sacra Teología.

sermons put into verse, questions of Holy Theology [put] into representable idea.

See *Obras completas,* ed. A. Valbuena Prat (Madrid, 1967), III, p. 427.

[23] Calderón, pp. 491-492.

> Come, pilgrims, come! Come, for this year the door is
> opening, which for so many ages and centuries had been
> closed. And since life is a journey for everyone, happy
> are those who through their pilgrimage deserve that this
> year spread through them the pious action and its holy
> reputation.

That is, the doors to Heaven were closed as a result of the original
sin, and man, shut out from Paradise, remained a wandering exile,
a *peregrino*, throughout this period. However, Christ's death on
the cross effected the reopening of the doors. Man, as a consequence, could not convert the aimless wandering of the *peregrinatio vitae* into a well-directed *peregrinatio* toward Heaven. The
only requirement was that he employ his free will judiciously and
choose the right path, the path of ascetic renunciation of the
world rather than of worldy indulgence, and that he not veer
from it. This path is arduous and full of spiritual obstacles, for
the devil himself, disguised as a *peregrino*, attempts to divert
El Hombre from his course. The latter is, however, saved through
the intervention of Amor divino and reaches his goal of Paradise.

El Hombre's arrival at the Gate of Heaven coincides concep-
tually with the pilgrim's arrival at the doors of St. Peter's Cathedral. El Hombre has undertaken the task of his salvation by means
of a spiritual *peregrinatio* and succeeded. The pilgrim through his
penitential journey likewise has achieved his eligibility to enter
Paradise more readily. His pilgrimage, like the spiritual *peregrinatio* of El Hombre, represents a conversion of the passive *peregrinatio vitae* into an active, meritorious *peregrinatio*.

Christ's PEREGRINATIO VITAE

This conversion would not have been possible had not Christ
through his life and death on earth effected the reopening of the
doors to salvation. Christ himself thus accomplished a *peregrinatio*
on earth. In Calderón's *auto, La cura y la enfermedad,* Christ,
under the name of El Peregrino, descends from Heaven in order
to heal *La Naturaleza Humana* which is ailing from sin. [24] We

---

[24] See *Obras completas,* III, 750 ff.

find the same concept in the writing of the Scottish vicar Samuel Purchas (ca. 1577-1626):

> Man by sinne [has] becomne a Worldly Pilgrime; Christ's Pilgrimage in the flesh [is an attempt] to recover him. [25]

Because of Christ's eminence his *peregrinatio* is the pincipal one:

> This was indeed the greatest of all peregrinations, when the word was made flesh and (leaving in a sort his heaven-ly country, and his Father's house) dwelt among us. The next remote peregrination was his ascension from the lower parts of the Earth (where also his life was a cer-taine uncertaine pilgrimage), farre above all heavens, to leade captivitie captive, and give gifts to Men (I, 317).

Because Christ's pilgrimage was the "greatest" it serves as a model for the rest of mankind. Christ tread the path through the world and proved that this path leads back to Heaven. All of mankind may now imitate Christ's *peregrinatio* and follow his footsteps. [26]

The association of Christ with the concept of *peregrinatio* had been a familiar one even long before the baroque period. It already occurs in Luke 24, 18, where the resurrected Christ appears to the disciples, walking with them to Emmaus in the guise of a stranger. Pretending not to know of the resurrection, he elicits their aston-ished commentary:

> Et respondens unus, cui nomen Cleophas, dixit ei: Tu solus peregrinus es in Ierusalem et non cognovisti quae facta sunt in illa his diebus?

> And the one of them, whose name was Cleophas, answer-ing said unto him, Art thou only a stranger in Jerusalem, and hast not known the things which are come to pass there in these days?

---

[25] Purchas, *His Pilgrimes*, I, 135.

[26] Christ's role as a model and a leader of mankind's *peregrini* is evident in *The Pilgrim's Progress*, where he is labelled "Prince of Pilgrims" (pp. 287, 300). The title of Déguileville's work *Le Pèlerinage Jesus Christ*, which is unavailable to me, likewise suggests such a model role in conjunction with *Le Pèlerinage de l'homme*.

Medieval writers frequently touch upon this scene. [27] In *Piers Plowman* (ca. 1370) in particular, Christ's characterization as a *peregrinus* is said to identify him with the poor:

> Why I moue this matere · is moste for the pore
> For in her lyknesse owre lorde · ofte hath ben y-knowne,
> Witnesse in the Paske-wyke · whan he ʒede to Emaus;
> Cleophas ne knewe hym nauʒte · that he Cryste were,
> For his pore paraille · and pylgrymes wedes,
> Tyl he blessed and brak · the bred that thei eten.
> So bi his werkes thei wisten · that he was Iesus. [28]

Because of Christ's precedence, poverty has been ennobled into a Christian virtue and represents a *peregrinatio* of its own. As a result, poverty became sought after by ascetic saints:

> Seynt Iohan and other seyntes · were seyne in pore clothynge,
> And as pore pilgrymes · preyed mennes godis (ll. 238-239).

PEREGRINATIO VITAE *and the Missionary*

The *peregrinatio* of Christ was thus open to various kinds of imitation. St. Basil already notes that the pursuit of the ascetic

---

[27] Among the English Wakefield Mystery Plays is one entitled *The Pilgrims,* in which Christ in the guise of a pilgrim appears to the Emmaus-bound Luke and Cleophas, who are likewise dressed as pilgrims. Not until he has broken the bread and disappeared do they realize his identity: "He was so like methought / to a pilgrim." See *The Wakefield Mystery Plays,* ed. Martial Rose (London, 1961), p. 411. This Biblical scene is also re-enacted in a repertory of Latin Easter plays, known as the *officium peregrinorum,* in which the priest-actors dress up in pilgrims' garb. See Otto Schüttpelz, "Die Erscheinungen vor den Emmausjüngern," *Germanistische Abhandlungen,* LXII (1930), 56-161.

In Spain Juan de Timoneda also constructed a play on this episode, entitled *Aucto del Castillo de Emaus,* in which Biblical personages mingle with characters from Spanish low-class society. Here Christ and his disciples appear dressed "com a romero," as pilgrims. And here too Cleophas addresses Christ as *peregrinus:*

> Y com, tu sols, peregri
> en Hierusalem viuies
> que no has vist estant alli
> les coses (mezqui de mi)
> que san seguit estos dies? (ll. 196-200)

See the edition by Mildred Edith Johnson in *Iowa Studies in Spanish Language and Literature,* IV (Iowa City, 1933), 15-42.

[28] *The Vision of William Concerning Piers the Plowman,* ed. W. W. Skeat (London, 1924), MS. B, Passus XI, ll. 224 ff.

life amounts to an imitation of Christ. [29] And for Thomas à Kempis the acknowledgement that life is a *peregrinatio* is an essential prerequisite for becoming a disciple of Christ. [30] On an earlier occasion we noted the statement of the French monk Friar Bieul who labels his missionary journey to the Orient a *peregrinatio*, asserting that he was inspired by the *peregrinatio* of Christ on earth. [31] Missionary activity thus became a form of tribute to Christ. This is emphatically evident in the accounts of the Irish monks who left in sizable numbers to serve as missionaries in Britain and on the continent under the motto of *peregrinari pro Christo*. [32] So close was their identification with the motto that frequently they would leave in groups of thirteen to imitate Christ and his disciples. [33] The disciples were, of course, the first followers of Christ, and they were also the first missionaries. St. Paul thus appropriately characterizes his apostolic journeys as *peregrinationes*. Speaking about the appointment of Titus to his staff, he notes:

> Misimus etiam cum illo fratrem, cuius laus est in evangelio per omnes ecclesias; non solum autem, sed et ordinatus est ab ecclesiis comes peregrinationis nostrae in hanc gratiam, quae ministratur a nobis ad Domini gloriam et destinatam voluntatem nostram (2. Cor. 8, 18-19).

---

[29] St. Basil's technical term for the ascetic imitation of Christ is Χριστοῦ μίμησις:

Ταπείνωσις, Χριστοῦ μίμησις. ἔπαρσις δὲ καὶ παρρησία καὶ ἀναίδεια, τοῦ διαβόλου μίμημα. Γίνου μιμητὴς Χριστοῦ, καὶ μὴ ἀντιχριστου.

Humility is an imitation of Christ. But conceit, audacity, and impudence are an imitation of the devil. Be an imitator of Christ, not of the antichrist!

Cited from *Sermo de renuntiatione saeculi*, PG, XXXI, 648.

[30]   Si vis debite stare & proficere, tene te exsulem & peregrinum super terram.

If you wish to achieve stability and merit, consider yourself an exile and pilgrim on earth.

De Imitatione Christi, Bk. I, Ch. 1.

[31] See our Chapter I.

[32] See Carl Selmers, ed., *Navigatio Sancti Brendani*, p. xxiii.

[33] See Fuhrmann, *Irish Monasteries*, p. 4.

And we have sent with him the brother, whose praise is
in the gospel throughout all the churches; and not that
only, but who was also chosen of the churches to travel
with us with his grace, which is administered by us to
the glory of the same Lord, and declaration of your
ready mind.

Succeeding missionaries could thus look back to prominent predecessors in their profession. While they were living in self-sought
exile carrying out their calling under often dangerous conditions,
they were comforted by the consciousness of identity with the
principal personalities of the Christian religion.

PEREGRINATIO VITAE *and* MILITIA CHRISTI

In our analysis so far we have concerned ourselves with the
effects which the concept of *peregrinatio vitae* had on the Christian tradition. In what follows we will explore the consequences
which arose out of this concept in combination with another idea,
that of the *militia Christi*. The close correspondence between them
is evident in the following passage by Henry, a twelfth-century
abbot of Clairvaux, who emphasizes the need for visible signs to
clarify abstract, spiritual facts:

> Et quia signis peregrinantes et militantes praecipue uti
> solent, recte peregrinanti et militanti civitati signa dan-
> tur. Quia quamdiu sumus in corpore, peregrinamur a
> Domino et quamdiu militia est hominis super terram,
> visibilium signorum scala ad visibilia necesse habemus
> uti.... [34]

> And since pilgrims and combatans are especially ac-
> customed to use signs, it is proper that signs are given to
> struggling pilgrim citizens. For as long as we dwell in
> the body, we are, like distant pilgrims, absent from God;
> and as long as struggle is the lot of man on earth we
> need to use a gamut of visible signs....

That is, man needs these signs because as long as he lives in his
state of *peregrinatio*, absent from God, his comprehension of

---

[34] *Tractatus de peregrinante civitate Dei,* in *PL,* CCXLI, 261.

abstractions is limited. For Henry, interestingly, the condition of *peregrinatio* also implies a *militia super terram,* which circumscribes man's earthly struggle; they are simultaneous conditions too of the *civitas Dei,* God's church on earth. [35]

The most prominent embodiment of the idea of *militia* is Job, who struggles to maintain his faith in the face of the trials and hardships which God visits upon him:

> Militia est vita hominis super terram, et, sicut dies mercenarii dies eius (Job 7, 1).

> Man's life on earth is a struggle, and his days are as [full of hardships as the] days of a soldier. [36]

At the same time he also embodies the adversities of the *peregrinatio* at their worst, and in the tradition of Christian thought he becomes the model of perseverance and fortitude. Like the *peregrinatio* the *militia* became a central concept of Christianity. The Roman catechism states that one becomes a *miles,* a soldier of God, as soon as one is baptized:

---

[35] The condition of *peregrinatio* is a fundamental ingredient of St. Augustine's concept of the *civitas Dei:*

> Gloriosissimam civitatem Dei, sive in hoc temporum cursu, cum inter impios peregrinatur ex fide vivens, sive in illa stabilitate sedis aeternae, quam nunc expectat per patientiam, quoadusque justitia convertatur in judicium deinceps adeptura per excellentiam victoria ultima et pace perfecta, hoc opere a te instituto, et mea promissione debito, defendere adversus eos qui Conditori ejus deos suso praeferunt, fili carissime Marcelline, suscepi (*PL,* XLI, Bk. I, Ch. 1).

> I have undertaken to defend the most glorious City of God against those who prefer their own gods over its founder. For the time being [the City] subsists by faith, living like a stranger among infidels, but patiently looking forward to its establishment in the eternal home, when righteousness will return to judgment and it will take eminent possession of it in final victory and perfect peace. This work — a fulfillment of a promise made to you, my dearest son Marcellinus — is great and difficult, but God will be my aide.

That is, in Heaven the Christian Church will find its final stability. But here on earth it exists in an uncertain condition of *peregrinatio* due to the onslaught of the pagan challenge. Because of this condition it is in need of defense, which Augustine proposes to undertake.

[36] We have provided our own translation here because the King James version departs considerably from the Vulgate: "It there not an appointed time to man upon earth? are not his days also like the days of an hireling?"

Qui baptizatus est, cum ab episcopo sacro chrismata
ungitur ... novae virtutis robore firmior atque adeo per-
fectus miles esse incipit. [37]

He who is baptized, as soon as he is anointed with the
holy oil by the bishop, is fortified with new vigor and
strength to become an altogether perfect soldier.

By coming into the world man automatically becomes a *peregrinus*;
but through baptism he also becomes a *miles*. Baptism is thus
seen as a vow, like a military oath of allegiance to the spiritual
army of Christ; that is, one joins the "Church militant." [38] To be
a Christian was thus synonymous with being a spiritual *miles
Dei*. The non-Christian, on the other hand, became known as a
paganus, a 'civilian' before God. [39]

There seemed to be no limit to which the military metaphor
could lend itself to elaboration. St. Paul, with his characteristic
inclination to render the abstract in as vivid terms as possible,
illustrates this trend in the following passage:

Propterea accipite armaturam Dei, ut possitis resistere in
die malo et in omnibus perfecti stare. State ergo succincti
lumbros vestros in veritate et induti loricam iustitiae et
calceati pedes in praeparatione evangelii paciis; in omnibus sumentes scutum fidei, in quo possitis omnia tela
nequissimi ignea extinguere. Et galeam salutis adsumitis
et gladium spiritus, quod est verbum Dei (Eph. 6, 13-
17).

Wherefore take unto you the whole armour of God, that
ye may be able to withstand in the evil day, and having
done all, to stand. Stand therefore, having your loins
girt about with truth, and having on the breastplate of
righteousness; and your feet shod with the preparation
of the gospel of peace; above all taking the shield of
faith, wherewith ye shall be able to quench all the fiery

---

[37] Cited from Adolf Harnack, *Militia Christi: Die christliche Religion
und der Soldatenstand in den ersten drei Jahrhunderten* (Tübingen, 1905),
p. 6.

[38] The term *sacramentum* which was applied to baptism originally meant
a secular military oath of allegiance. See Harnack, p. 34.

[39] Harnack, p. 68.

darts of the wicked. And take the helmet of salvation, and the sword of the Spirit, which is the word of God.

In St. Paul's opinion, then, the Christian requires an armor made up of the various virtues to fortify himself against the assault of evil. This thought was frequently recalled in Christian literature. We find it, for example, in *Le Pèlerinage de l'homme* by Guillaume de Déguileville. Here Grace Dieu advises the *pèlerin* bound to the celestial Jerusalem to don a military outfit:

> 'ffyrst, to make thy syluen strong.
> To be myghty a-geyn al wrong,
> Yt be-houeth, in thy diffence,
> ffor to makë resistence,
> That thow hauë strong armure.
> And ffyrst, (thy syluen to assure,)
> Next thy body shal be set
> A purpoynt or a doublet,
> On wych thow shalt fful myghtyly
> Be gyrt and stryned ryht strongly
> 'With a gyrdel off Ryhtwysnesse,
> Ther-on thyn armure for to dresse.' [40]

Similarly in John Bunyan's work *The Pilgrim's Progress* (1678) Christian is shown the armor which stands ready for the pilgrims in the Palace of Beautiful:

> The next day they had him (Christian) into the Armoury; where they shewed him all manner of Furniture, which the Lord had provided for Pilgrims, as Sword, Shield, Helmet, Breastplate, *All-Prayer,* and Shooes that would not wear out. And there was here enough of this to harness out as many men for the service of their Lord as there be Stars in the Heaven for multitude. [41]

---

[40] For lack of a French edition I cite from *The Pilgrimage of the Life of Man,* trans. John Lydgate (London, 1899), p. 202.

[41] *The Pilgrim's Progress,* ed. Roger Sharrock (Oxford, 1960), p. 54. For further occurrences of the topos *lorica* see Samuel C. Chew, *The Pilgrimage of Life* (New Haven and London, 1962), pp. 140-143. For the Romance literatures in particular consult Felix Lecoy, *Récherches sur le "Libro de buen amor"* (Paris, 1938), pp. 184-187.

In all of these instances *militia* appears as a concommittant of *peregrinatio* to circumscribe an attitude of spiritual preparedness. As we have seen, Christians tended to convert passive principle of the Biblical *peregrinatio vitae* into an active working concept. We may ask therefore to what extent the *militia* too could be turned into an applied principle. This tendency is in fact already noticeable in St. Paul, who identifies his fellow missionaries as *commilitones*, [42] thus giving the concept of *militia* a notable extension. The ordinary Christian is a *miles Dei* only in the sense that he fights off the vices of the world which threaten his spiritual integrity. His *militia* is therefore a defensive concept. The missionary, on the other hand, not only stands up for his faith but also attempts to impose it on others through persuasion. His profession thus incorporates a degree of aggressiveness stemming from a heartfelt conviction which does not recoil at worldly obstacles of any kind.

This aggressive spirituality is abundantly reflected in St. Ignatius of Loyola (1491-1556). In his autobiography, reputedly dictated by him, he calls himself *el peregrino*. [43] Since he employs the term even after he has accomplished his pilgrimage to Jerusalem, it appears that he meant to describe in a far broader sense his exclusive dedication to a Christian cause, his ascetic development. He first conceived the idea for his calling through the haphazard reading of Saints' lives while he lay wounded. These books, however, did not provide his exclusive reading material. He also read many books of chivalry, to which, like many of his contemporaries, he was greatly addicted. Although he later came to deplore his taste for these books, he never quite escaped their influence. He was, after all, himself a soldier who admired the tales of knightly

---

[42] In Philippians 2, 25 he characterizes a fellow missionary as a *commilito*, a 'fellow-soldier':

> Necessarium autem existimavi Epaphroditum fratrem et cooperatorem et commilitonem meum, vestrum autem apostulum et ministrum necessitatis meae mittere ad vos.

> Yet I supposed it necessary to send you Epaphroditus, my brother, and companion in labour, and fellow-soldier, but your messenger, and he that ministered to my wants.

[43] See *Obras completas de San Ignacio de Loyola*, ed. I. Iparraguirre (Madrid, 1952), for example on pp. 39, 62, 64.

prowess. The ceremonies with which he initiates his ascetic career reflect this influence:

> Y como tenía todo el entendimento lleno de aquellas cosas, Amadís de Gaula y de semejantes libros, veníanle algunas al pensamiento semejantes a aquéllas; y así se determinó de velar sus armas toda una noche, sin sentarse ni acostarse, mas a ratos en pie y a ratos de rodillas, delante el altar de Nuestra Señora de Monserrate, adonde tenía determinado dejar sus vestidos y vestir las armas de Christo. Pues, partido de este lugar... concertó con el confesor que mandase recoger la mula y que la espada y el puñal colgase en la iglesia en el altar de nuestra Señora (pp. 40-41).

> And as he had his mind full of such things as the *Amadis de Gaula* and similar books, other similar thoughts came to him. And so he decided to watch his arms all night long, without sitting or lying down, but rather at times standing up or kneeling before the altar of Our Lady of Monserrate, where he had decided to leave his clothes and to dress in the armour of Christ. Then, on leaving this place, he persuaded the confessor to send for the mule and to allow him to hang the sword and the knife in the church on the altar of Our Lady.

That is, he sheds his soldier's outfit and exchanges it for the "arms of Christ," the pilgrim's garb. He is now in fact, "el nuevo soldado de Christo" (p. 44). The martial undertone of his philosophy would eventually shape his whole outlook: he set out to conquer the minds and hearts of his prospective followers, forming them into the quasimilitary Compañía de Jesús and compelling them to undergo strenuous *ejercicios*.

In Loyola, then, the idea of worldly knighthood produced a spiritual knighthood. This transformation succeeded because the militant attitude was already contained in the ascetic *peregrinatio* which he undertook. The secular idea thus did not in fact create the militant spirit; it merely reinforced it with forms and symbols. To what extent this reinforcement may go is exemplified in the modern phenomenon of the Salvation Army. Here the designations of modern armies have been adopted to the point of saturation, complete with ranks and uniforms. Its slogans, too, are borrowed from the military:

Heroic enterprises yet undreamed of beckon the new pilgrims, who, through Officership, will take the high road of self-denial, dedicating themselves as consecrated technicians for fresh adventures in faith. [44]

Here too we note the impact of the forms of secular warfare reinforcing the already existing spiritual militancy, the *militia Dei* which is contained within the concept of *peregrinatio*. The Salvation Army officer embodies the hardships of the militant *peregrinatio*; he is himself a pilgrim. So emphatic is the consciousness of his position that it also finds its way into the Salvation Army Songbook:

I'm a pilgrim and a stranger, rough and thorny is the road;
Often in the midst of danger, but it leads me on to God. [45]

Yet we must not compare the *peregrinatio* of the Salvation Army officer with that of the Jesuit Loyola. The latter as a Catholic believes emphatically in salvation through works, that is, through his ascetic *ejercicios* he may hope to gain entrance to Paradise. Protestants generally deemphasize, and in the cases of radical reformers like Calvin, disavow the validity of the doctrine of salvation through works. For them the meritorious *peregrinatio* of asceticism has consequently little value. It was, after all, the result of Catholic tradition and had not been endorsed by the Bible. The Protestant concept is therefore limited to the original *peregrinatio vitae* of the Bible, which represents a state of consciousness rather than a working principle. The Salvation Army officer, too, performs good works but these are primarily intended to enhance the salvation of his fellow men through the alleviation of unbearable social conditions which breed sin. But unlike the Catholic he may not believe that these works will result in direct credit towards his own salvation. His pilgrimage then is not an ascetic, meritorious *peregrinatio*. For him the meaning of *peregri-*

---

[44] Don Pitt, *Pilgrim's Progress: 20th Century. The Story of Salvation Army Officership* (New York, 1950), p. 50. Note also the following passage on p. 59: "Other veterans have 'died in action' — on Salvation Army platforms while witnessing the wonders of salvation. Many have expressed the wish that they might have such a valiant ending to their long pilgrimage."

[45] Cited from Pitt, p. 46.

natio is limited to its function as a convenient metaphor to size up the hardships of life. He seeks out these hardships deliberately and therefore possesses a heightened consciousness of them.

In both the Compañía de Jesús and the Salvation Army we have noted how the idea of secular warfare reactivated and reinforced the idea of spiritual warfare, the *militia Christi*, and that it did so within the scope of the concept of *peregrinatio*. The result was the establishment of an aggressive spirituality placed at the service of God and working to enhance the salvation of others. Worldly and spiritual warfare thus thrive on a similar state of mind, even though they differ in that the former translates a mental attitude into physical violence. In view of this correspondence one wonders to what extent the two ideas may influence each other. If secular warfare may kindle a spiritual one, may the spiritual *militia* in turn inspire a worldly one? The Jesuits, indeed, have been known to enter the political struggle.

PEREGRINATIO *and Secular Warfare*

In its beginnings the *militia Christi* was confined strictly to the spiritual sphere. St. Paul affirms this adamantly:

> Induite vos armaturam Dei, ut possitis stare adversus insidias diaboli. Quoniam non est nobis colluctio adversus carnem et sanguinem, sed adversus principes et potestates, adversus mundi rectores tenebrarum harum, contra spiritualia nequitiae in caelestibus (Eph. 6, 11-12).

> Put on the whole armour of God, that ye may be able to stand against the devil. For we wrestle not against flesh and blood, but against principalities, against powers, against the rulers of the darkness of this world, against spiritual wickedness in high places.

Killing was simply out of the question for the Christian; the fifth commandment forbade it. The early Christian would therefore evade the armed services if he could do so. Eventually, however, Christianity did enter the Roman army through the conversion of soldiers who managed to make their new religion compatible with their profession. There must have been a considerable number of Christians in Constantine's army to allow him to adopt the Christian banner so readily. Thus, curiously enough, it was in the army that the decisive changeover to Christianity occurred. With Constantine's victory secular warfare had become acceptable to Christian thought, and was indeed regarded as holy if it furthered the cause of Christianity. [46]

The holiest of wars in the history of Christianity were, of course, the crusades. Around the year 1000 many pilgrims flocked to the Holy Land in expectation of the millennium during which Christ had promised to return. At the same time Muslim policies towards Christians became more intransigent; pilgrims were harrassed and obliged to defend themselves with arms. As a rule though, pilgrims were obliged to be unarmed. [47] The policy of Pope Urban II, however, changed this. Eager to help the cause of Christendom triumph over Islam, Urban could not help viewing the pilgrimages as a form of misplaced, ineffectual devotion. In 1089, therefore, he urged the noblemen of Catalonia not to waste their efforts on pilgrimages but rather to proceed to the defense of Tarragona. In return he promised the same indulgences which were customarily given to pilgrims. [48] In the Council of Clermont, moreover, he promised total remission of sins to anyone who would go to Jerusalem to free the Holy Sepulcher. [49] The pilgrimage to Jerusalem now became an armed pilgrimage. Accordingly, Fulcher of Chartres, a chronicler of the first crusade, states that the Franks "ordained by God, made an armed pilgrimage to Jerusalem" *(Dei ordinatione cum armis Jerusalem peregrinati sunt).* [50] The ceremonies of the crusading pledges likewise resembled those given to pilgrims. The officiating priest would bless not only the pilgrim's staff and pouch, but also his sword. [51] From then on, *peregrinus* became a common designation for the crusader.

Eventually, however, the idea of the crusade outgrew its close ties with the pilgrimage. Crusades were soon undertaken in other

---

[46] Harnack, *Militia Christi,* pp. 86-87.

[47] Carl Erdmann, *Die Entstehungsgeschichte des Kreuzzugsgedankens* (Stuttgart, 1955), p. 281.

[48] Erdmann, p. 292.

[49] Erdmann, pp. 294, 316-317.

[50] *Historia Hierosolymitana,* in *PL,* CLV, 823. Other crusading chronicles use the same terminology.

[51] Erdmann, p. 307.

parts of the world, such as Eastern Europe where the Teutonic order began to establish its sway over the pagans. Nevertheless, the knights of this order were also identified as *peregrini* in documents of that period. [52] A knight of that order would pledge his whole life to his pursuit. He was, therefore, a *peregrinus* by profession similar to the *peregrinus*-monk, and like the latter he too could expect his chances of salvation to increase by virtue of his profession. By dint of his works he could enter Paradise.

In the concept of *peregrinatio* the church had found a powerful inducement for rallying the arms of Christendom for its purposes. It could be invoked whenever the need for a "holy" war arose in later times. In Britain, for example, several Scottish counties rose up against the reformer-king Henry VIII in 1536. The armed insurrection was termed an *Itinerarium Gratiae*, which in its translated form also became known as the "Pilgrimage of Grace." [53] Finally, a remnant of the idea is still perceivable in the following German army song of World War I:

> Nikolaus, du frommer, du heiliger Man,
> Du Friedenfürst der Welten, wir kommen nun heran,
> Dir ein Loblied zu singen mit Pulver und mit Blei,
> Auf dass es schön tut klingen bis in die Mandschurei.
>
> Ihr Deutschen allzusammen, nun habet guten Mut,
> Die Wallfahrt soll gelingen uns wohl in Gottes Hut:
> Mit Kanon und Flinte spielet wacker auf,
> Dem heil'gen Mann zu Ehren und seinem Russenhauf. [54]

>> Nicholaus, you pious, holy man; you, the world's prince of peace, behold we are approaching now to sing you a devotional song with powder and lead, [so loud] that it may ring out as far as Manchuria.

>> All you Germans, take courage, with God's protection this pilgrimage will succeed: strike up the music with cannons and guns in honor of the holy man and his band of Russians.

---

[52] See Walter Hubatsch, *Quellen zur Geschichte des Deutschen Ordens* (Göttingen, 1954), pp. 58, 76.

[53] See Madelaine Hope Dodds and Ruth Dodds, *The Pilgrimage of Grace 1536-37 and the Exeter Conspiracy 1538*, 2 vols. (Cambridge, 1915).

[54] Cited from Winfried Elbers, *Das deutsche Soldatenlied im 1. Weltkrieg und seine publizistiche Bedeutung* (Essen, 1963), pp. 80-81.

Here Czar Nicholas is portrayed as the saint to whom the Germans will make a *Wallfahrt,* a 'pilgrimage,' and they will play for him a *Loblied,* a 'devotional song' with the sound of guns. The song is of course a parody, intended to caricaturize the enemy. A serious undertone persists, however. It consists in the rallying cry which employs the terminology of the *peregrinatio*-crusade as an expression of a national fervor, testifying thereby to the power of an idea which had survived for over 800 years.

Perhaps the best measure of its power is the tribute that was paid to it in works of fiction. The most renowned elaboration of the crusade ideal is Torquato Tasso's epic *La Gerusalemme liberata* (1580), which describes the siege and conquest of the Holy City by an army lead by Godfrey of Bouillon. Godfrey's foe is the Sultan Soliman, whose kingdom suffers as a result of the Christian invasion:

> ...poi che contra i turchi e gli altri infidi
> passâr ne l'Asia l'arme peregrine,
> fur sue terre espugnate, ed ei sconfitto
> ben fu due fiate in general conflitto. [55]

> ...when the pilgrim army came to Asia [to fight] against the Turks and other infidels his [i.e., Soliman's] lands were ravaged, and he was defeated twice in all-out battle.

---

[55] *La Gerusalemme liberata,* IX, 4. Lope de Vega wrote an epic poem on the same theme with the title *La Jerusalén conquistada* in which he causes — with considerable poetic license — Alfonso VIII, the victor of the battle of Las Navas, to ally with Richard the Lion Heart for a crusade. Here too the crusaders are characterized as *peregrini:*

> Yo canto el celo y las hazañas canto
> de aquel varón, soldado y peregrino
> que a ser del Asia universal espanto
> desde la selva Caledonia vino;
> el que el tirano del Sepulcro santo
> venció en los campos del Belén divino
> haciendo a un tiempo (de Minerva infusas)
> llorar las armas y cantar las musas (I, 1).

I sing of the zeal and I sing of the deeds of that courageous man, soldier and pilgrim who, coming from the forests of Caledonia, struck universal fear into Asia; the one who in the lands of Bethlehem defeated the tyrant occupying the Holy Sepulcher, [and]

Here the term *arme peregrine* signifies the invading foreign armies. However, it also makes an oblique reference to the pilgrim status of the crusaders. This is pointed out in the concluding stanza of the poem where Godfrey after taking the city approaches the Holy Sepulcher to fulfill his vow like a pilgrim:

> Così vince Goffredo; ed a lui tanto
> avanza ancor de la diurna luce,
> ch'a la città già liberata, al santo
> ostel di Cristo i vincitor conduce.
> Né pur deposto il sanguinoso manto,
> viene al tempio con gli altri il sommo duce;
> e qui l'arme sospende, e qui devoto
> il gran Sepolcro adora; e scioglie il voto (XX, 144).

> Thus Godfrey conquered. And there is still enough daylight left for him to lead the saintly host of Christ to the now liberated city. Without taking off his bloodied coat the supreme leader arrives at the temple with the others, and hanging up his weapons there he prays at the Sepulcher and fulfills his vow.

Godfrey's crusade, like a pilgrimage, is a meritorious *peregrinatio*, and as such it deserves the reward of Paradise. This reward is promised to him in a dream by the apparition of a fallen comrade. Pointing out to him the amenities of Paradise, the deceased declares:

> Questo è tempio di Dio: qui son le sedi
> de' suoi guerrieri: e tu avrai loco in queste (XIV, 7).

> This is the abode of God: here are the loges of his warriors, and you will have a place among them.

In Tasso's poem, then, the *peregrinatio*-crusade comprises the central theme. This feature distinguishes his epic from the *Orlando Furioso* (1516) of his renowned predecessor Ariosto. Both poems draw for their plots on the medieval repertory of the romances

---

who, under the inspiration of Minerva, made the arms weep and the muses sing at one [and the same] time.
Cited from *Obras escogidas*, ed. F. C. Sainz de Robles (Madrid, 1946).

and even employ some of the same characters. Each author, however, uses this material in a different manner. Ariosto's outstanding achievement consisted in transforming the originally oral material into a literary epic. At the same time he accompanied this conversion with an innovative tone by puncturing the unself-conscious heroic stance of the medieval characters with a refined form of irony. Compared with its medieval sources the *Orlando Furioso* is thus far more sophisticated; through it the medieval romance has become the epic of the Renaissance living room.

Yet the *Orlando* fared badly at the hands of the Inquisition, which condemned much of its sensual exuberance. [56] The *Gerusalemme* likewise did not escape criticism. But the poem had one feature which was bound to endear it to the Church: it presented the Church at its most glorious and most militant in the conquest of Jerusalem. The *Orlando* lacks this theme; its characters concern themselves only with each other, with their loves and their combats. The characters in the *Gerusalemme*, too, concern themselves with personal affairs. Nevertheless, they do have an overriding preoccupation which ultimately subordinates their personal activities, namely the theme of the crusade. In spite of occasional relapses into more egoistic pursuits, the knights feel committed to a Christian cause, a cause for which they pledged themselves by becoming *peregrini*, 'warriors of Christ.'

As the characters are committed, so is the poem itself. By portraying the medieval knight as a defender of the faith, with his prowess bridled by a Christian cause, it showed him in the role in which the official Church liked to see him most. During the Counter Reformation such commitment was especially appreciated, not only because it harmonized with that era's reawakened spirituality, but also because the literary portrayal of knighthood which proliferated in the course of the sixteenth century was a continuous source of apprehensions for the church. In its form of the prose romance the nature of the portrayals had become increasingly extravagant and heedless to moral and esthetic

---

[56] The Portuguese Inquisition placed the Italian version on the *Index* in 1581. In Spain it appeared on the *Index* for the first time in 1612. See Giovanni M. Bertini, "L'*Orlando Furioso* e l'Inquisizione Spagnuola," *Convivium*, VII (1935), 540-550.

dimensions. The crude sensualism, the unorthodox miracles, and the very wildest of other improbabilities which inept imitators often concocted and passed off in the name of chivalry frequently offended even moderate good taste, not to speak of the Inquisition's severe sense of morality. There were, of course, exceptional romances portraying knights of exemplary virtue, such as the original *Amadís de Gaula* (1508). The perceptive reader thus could not but adopt an ambiguous attitude towards the chivalric genre. He would appreciate wholeheartedly the portrayal of the knight's devotion, of his virtue and of his bravery which characterized some of the romances. But if he had only a reasonably critical mind he would view with distaste the excesses of phantasy in which others indulged. The primary cause for this exorbitant, flourishing fantasy was the fact that real chivalry no longer existed. The chivalric romance constituted a hermetic world of its own, sealed off from the contemporary world of the writer as well as of the reader. Neither of the two was therefore able to verify in the realm of reality those things which he wrote or read in the book. There were thus no critical standards for curtailing the imagination, with the result that the imagination was allowed to run wild.

Don Quijote *and Spiritual Knighthood*

This problem was sensed very acutely by Cervantes who gave his preoccupations an artistic expression in his novel *Don Quijote*. The question of whether or not Cervantes intended to demolish the vogue of the chivalric romance has excited critics of many generations. Actually, Cervantes himself reserves for himself an attitude of ambiguity. The debate about the romances between the Canon and the priest in Chapter 48 ranges from a condemnation of misguided fantasy to a eulogy of the genre's potential as an instrument for teaching virtue. The character of Don Quijote himself dramatizes this ambiguity. The exorbitant fantasies of the romances have shattered his wit, and his attempt to embody the now anachronistic way of life of the knight-errant appears as both mad and hilarious to the bystander as well as to the reader.

Cervantes, however, does not content himself with the perspective of a bystander; he also delves into the interior of Don

Quijote's motivation, which at closer scrutiny appears as very respectable. To begin with, we note that Don Quijote calls his pursuit of knighthood a *peregrinatio:*

> Mucho me pesa, Sancho, que hayas dicho y digas que yo fuí el que te saqué de tus casillas, sabiendo que yo no me quedé en mis casas: juntos salimos, juntos fuimos y juntos peregrinamos; una misma fortuna y una misma suerte ha corrido por los dos: si a ti te mantearon una vez, a mí me han molido ciento, y esto es lo que te llevo de ventaja (II, 2).

> It grieves me much, Sancho, that you should have said, and are saying, that it was I who drew you away from your cabin, knowing well that I did not remain at home [myself]. We departed together, we went together, we journeyed together. The same fortune and the same lot has accompanied us: while you were tossed in a blanket once, I was beaten a hundred times, and in this respect I have an advantage over you.

In one sense the *peregrinatio* of Don Quijote refers to the misguided imitation of knight-errantry, in the course of which he and Sancho have been battered and bruised. The incidents in which they incurred their injuries appear as riotously comic to the bystander, just as the whole of Don Quijote's pursuit is comic. However, seen from the vantage point of Don Quijote the *peregrinatio* is motivated by a serious aim: he sees it as the reliving of the ascetic *peregrinatio* whose narrow path the Christian warrior is treading:

> yo inclinado de mi estrella voy por la angosta senda de la caballería andante, por cuyo exercicio desprecio la hacienda, pero no la honra (II, 32).

> Guided by [the influence of] my star I go along the narrow path of knight-errantry, and for the sake of its exercise I despise possessions, but not honor.

For Don Quijote, then, the exercise of chivalry is an ascetic *peregrinatio.* As such it is equivalent to the ascetic *peregrinatio* of the monk. In the following passage Don Quijote discusses this equivalence with Sancho, who is the first speaker:

—Así que, señor mío, más vale ser un humilde fraile-
cito, de cualquier orden que sea, que valiente y andante
caballero; más alcanzan con Dios dos docenas de discipli-
nas que dos mil lanzadas, ora las den a gigantes, ora a
vestiglos, o a endrigos.

—Todo eso es así —respondió don Quijote—; pero no
todos podemos ser frailes, y muchos son los caminos por
donde lleva Dios los suyos al cielo: religión es la caballe-
ría; caballeros santos hay en la gloria (II, 8).

"Therefore my lord, to be a humble little friar of
whatever order is more worthy than being a courageous
knight-errant. Two dozen lashes influence God more than
two thousand lance-thrusts, be they dealt against giants,
monsters or dragons."

"This is all quite so," answered Don Quijote, "but we
cannot all be friars, and the paths whereby God draws his
favorites to Heaven are many: chivalry is a religion, there
are saintly knights in the glory [of Heaven]."

In Don Quijote's view, then, the roads leading to Paradise are
numerous. Since Paradise is gained through a meritorious *peregrinatio* on earth, each of the roads constitutes a *peregrinatio* of its
own which fulfills the entrance requirement to Heaven. The ascetic
monk accomplishes this by disciplining his body, the Christian
knight through his self-sought hardships sustained in the service
of his calling. [57]

---

[57] In Guillén de Castro's play *Las mocedades del Cid* (1618), Rodrigo
affirms that each of these roads, including that of knighthood, is appropriate
for the *peregrino* (*Clásicos Castellanos*, XV, vv. 2167 ff.):

Para general consuelo
de todos, la mano diestra
de Dios mil caminos muestra,
y por todos se va al cielo.
Y assí, el que fuere guiado
por el mundo peregrino,
ha de buscar el camino
que diga con el estado.
Para el bien que promete
de un alma limpia y sencilla,
lleve el frayle su capilla,
y el clérigo su bonete,
y su capote doblado
lleve el tosco labrador,
que quiça acierta mejor
por el surco de su arado.

Because the two types of *peregrinationes* are equivalent, they are also interchangeable. That is, the most perfect of the knights may become saints, as did St. George:

> Este caballero fue uno de los mejores andantes que tuvo la milicia divina; llamóse San Jorge, y fue además defendedor de doncellas (II, 58).

> This knight was one of the best knights-errant which the Divine host possessed; his name was Saint George, and besides, he was a protector of damsels.

St. George's knighthood is a twofold one. On the one hand he is a typical *caballero andante* whose profession includes the rescuing of damsels. On the other hand his knighthood also has a spiritual component; like the ascetic monk he is a *miles dei*. [58] Both aspects are integral parts of true knight-errancy.

> Y el soldado y cavallero,
> si lleva buena intención,
> con dorada guarnición,
> con plumas en el sombrero,
>   a cavallo, y con dorada
> espuela, galán divino,
> si no es que yerra el camino
> hará bien esta jornada;
>   porque al cielo caminando
> ya llorando, ya riendo
> van los unos padeciendo,
> y los otros peleando.

To everyone's general consolation, God's right hand points out a thousand paths, and on all of them one [may] go to Heaven.

And so, he who would be guided like a pilgrim through the world has to search for the path which corresponds to his station [in life].

For [the purpose of attaining] the promised reward of a pure and simple soul let the monk wear his hood, the cleric his cap,

And [let] the coarse peasant [wear] his folded cape, for perhaps he succeeds best by the furrow of his plow.

And the soldier and knight, if he is well-intentioned, decorated with gilded harness, with feathers in his hat,

On horseback, and with gilded spurs, a divine gallant man, if he does not stray from his path, will accomplish his journey well;

For, whether weeping or laughing, some walk to Heaven suffering, some fighting.

[58] The full extent of the knight's participation in the spiritual *militia* is seen by the fact that the angels themselves constitute a *militia caelestis* (Luke 2, 13). During the Middle Ages, moreover, the archangel Michael

If knights may be saints, then saints may also be knights. This is the status which Don Quijote attributes to St. Paul:

> Éste fue el mayor enemigo que tuvo la Iglesia de Dios Nuestro Señor en su tiempo, y el mayor defensor suyo que tendrá jamás; caballero andante por la vida, y santo a pie quedo por la muerte, trabajador incansable en la viña del señor. . . . (II, 58).

> This was the greatest enemy that the Church of God our Lord had, and the greatest champion that it will ever have. A knight-errant in life and a steadfast saint in death, a tireless worker in the Lord's vineyard. . . .

St. Paul, of course, was not a real knight; the status of *caballero andante* thus applied to him refers to his emphatically professed spiritual warfare, the *militia Dei*. In Don Quijote's conception, then, there is a complete fusion of spiritual knighthood with virtuous worldly knighthood. Because Don Quijote, too, professes a virtuous chivalry, he too may claim allegiance to the spiritual warriors, St. George and St. Paul, although as a sinner he may not claim their status of sainthood:

> . . . estos santos y caballeros profesaron lo que yo profeso, que es el ejercicio de las armas; sino que la diferencia que hay entre mí y ellos es que ellos fueron santos y pelearon a lo divino, y yo soy pecador y peleo a lo humano (II, 58).

> . . . these saints and knights professed what I profess, which is the exercise of arms. But the difference between me and them is that they were saints and fought in a divine fashion, and I am a sinner and fight in a human fashion.

It is this dual nature of the concept of knighthood which Cervantes needed to consider in his evaluation of the chivalric romances. He realized that the comprehensive notion of knighthood included more than armor, horse and lance. These manifestations were, after all, anachronistic in his time. But the spiritual

---

was thought to have originated worldly knighthood. See Huizinga, *The Waning of the Middle Ages*, p. 67.

component of knighthood needed no such externals because it consisted above all in an attitude. [59] It was the spiritual chivalry which motivated the *peregrinatio* of Loyola, and which inspired his founding of the Compañía de Jesús. Spiritual chivalry thus possessed great relevance in the time of Cervantes. Through the Jesuits, who became the leaders of the Counter Reformation, the ideal of spiritual warfare in the service of a militant church permeated and dominated an entire epoch. It is often said that Spain in the Golden Age had never quite shed the spirit of the Middle Ages. [60] This would seem to hold true with respect to the notion of chivarly. If France produced the first flowering of chivalry, then Spain produced the last. The spiritual knighthood of the Counter Reformation was its most pertinent and historically the most potent expression. And in this form it was certainly not anachronistic. Cervantes recognized this, and he knew that a semblance of spiritual chivalry was to a degree perpetuated through the medium of the chivalric romance. Loyola, after all, modelled his spiritual knighthood on the reading of these romances. Unfortunately, however, the romances cluttered the spiritual ideal with a stifling superstructure of badly conceived and wildly imagined externals. In *Don Quijote* Cervantes endeavors to sort out the central notion of spiritual chivalry, and to rescue it by separating it from these anachronistic externals. In the figure of Don Quijote he consigned these anachronisms to the inferno of ridicule. Don Quijote is at his maddest whenever he plunges into one of his anachronistic feats, whereas he is remarkably sane and

---

[59] How readily the chivalric concept of the romances was associated with the spiritual *militia* is evidenced by the appearance of divinized versions of these romances. In these versions, too, the spiritual knighthood is characterized as a *peregrinatio*. This is seen in the following titles which I cite from Vilanova, "El peregrino andante," p. 111: Pedro Hernández de Villaumbrales, *El caballero del Sol o sea la Peregrinación de la vida del hombre puesto en batalla* (Medina del Campo, 1552). Also Fray Alonso de Soria, *Historia y milicia cristiana del caballero Peregrino* (Cuenca, 1601).

[60]   Spain does not turn its back on the Middle Ages on entering the sixteenth century (as France does); rather without shutting itself off from contemporary influences it continues the tradition of the Middle Ages.

Translated from Dámaso Alonso, *Poesía de la Edad Media y poesía de tipo tradicional* (Buenos Aires, 1942), p. 9.

rational whenever he expounds in rational terms the central ideas of spiritual chivalry. It is interesting to note that when at last he sheds his madness, he also sheds his credence in whatever he believed in during his moments of most acute spells of madness. That is, he disavows, not the spiritual part of chivalry, but the anachronistic externals which the romances mistakenly claimed to be the essence of knighthood:

> Yo tengo juicio ya, libre y claro, sin las sombras caligino-sas de la ignorancia que sobre él me pusieron mi amarga y continua leyenda de los detestables libros de caballería. Ya conozco sus disparates y sus embelecos, y no me pesa sino que este desengaño ha llegado tan tarde. .... (II, 74).

> I have now regained my judgement; it is free and clear without the ashen shadows of ignorance which the bitter and continuous reading of the detestable books of chivalry imposed on me. Now I have come to know their folly and fraud and I am only sorry that this recognition has come so late....

Don Quijote condemns the books of chivalry because they have driven him into the erroneous assumption that they represent the essence, the spiritual component of knighthood. They have buried this essential idea of knighthood under a maze of "disparates and embelecos," of misconceived and misconstrued externals. On the other hand he does not include in his condemnation those ideas of chivalry that he held when he was rational, among which the idea of spiritual chivalry ranked foremost. Unwittingly or not, he allows it to escape his severe censure, so that, significantly perhaps, it survives the process of elimination.

Cervantes, it seems, did not so much intend to destroy the validity of knighthood by his censure of the chivalric romances. Rather he wished to reappraise it, to discriminate between what was relevant in his time and what was irrelevant. By this process he was able to isolate and bring into relief the essence of knighthood, the *militia Christi* of St. Paul, St. George and St. Ignatius, which forms a part of Don Quijote's *peregrinatio*.

The Protestant Concept of PEREGRINATIO VITAE

Christian knighthood, then, constitutes one more illustration of the application of the principle of *peregrinatio vitae*. Like the ascetic monk and the devotionary pilgrim, the knight too is engaged in a meritorious *peregrinatio,* whose end is the attainment of Paradise. We have seen that the original Biblical concept of *peregrinatio* was a passive one, and that it was only through tradition that the passive concept became an active one through which salvation could be attained. The belief that one may attain salvation through the work of one's own effort is the outstanding characteristic of Roman Catholicism, and it was the greatest point of controversy for Reformation critics who preferred the authority of the Bible over Church tradition. One of the most radical critics of that belief was Calvin (1509-1564). In the following passage he too addresses himself to this principle:

> Talibus rudimentis probe nos simul instituit Scriptura quis rectus sit bonorum terrestrium vsus: res in componenda vitae ratione minime neglegenda. Nam si viuendum est, vtendum quoque necessariis vitae adminiculiis. Nec fugere ea quoque possumus quae videntur oblectationi magis quam necessitati inseruire. Modum ergo tenere oportet, vt pura conscientia siue ad necessitatem siue oblectamentum vtamur. Eum Dominus verbo suo praescribit, quum docet, viam praesentem quandam peregrinationem suis esse, qua in caeleste regnum contendunt. Si per terram transeundum est duntaxat, non dubium quin eatenus vtendum sit eius bonis, vt cursum nostrum iuuent potius quam morentur. Ideo non abs re suadet Paulus hoc mundo ita vtendum esse quasi non vtamur: eodem animo emendas esse possessiones quo venduntur. Verum quia lubricus est hic locus, & vtranque in partem procliuis ad lapsum, studeamus pedem figere vbi tuto stare liceat. Fuerunt enim nonnulli, boni & sancti alioqui homines, qui quum viderent intemperiem ac luxuriam effraeni libidine perpetuo euagire nisi seuerius coerceatur, corrigere autem tam periculosum malum cuperent: quae una illis ocurrebat ratio, corporeis bonis vti homini permiserunt, quatenus necessitatis interesset. Pium quidem consilium: sed impendio austeriores fuerunt. Nam (quod est valde

periculosum) arctiores laqueos induerunt conscientiis quam quibus verbo Domini stringerentur. [61]

By such rudiments the Scripture at the same time instructs us well in the proper use of earthly blessings, a subject which in forming a scheme of life is by no means to be neglected. For if we are to live, we must use the necessary supports of life. Nor can we avoid even those things which seem to serve pleasure more than necessity. We must therefore observe a middle way, so that we may use them with a clear conscience, whether for necessity or for pleasure. This the Lord prescribes by His word, when He tells us that to His people the present journey [of life] is a kind of pilgrimage by which they hasten to the Heavenly kingdom. If we are only to pass through the earth, there can be no doubt that we are to use its blessings only insofar as they assist our progress, rather than retard. It is therefore not in vain that Paul admonishes us to use this world as if we were not using it, and to buy possessions as if we were selling them. For, since this is a slippery place, and there is great danger of falling on either side, let us endeavor to fix our feet where we can stand safely. There have been some otherwise good and holy men who, when they saw intemperance and unbridled luxury perpetually carried to excess, wanted, if not to severely curb, at least to correct such a dangerous evil by allowing men to use physical blessings only insofar as they were necessary: a pious advice indeed, but unneccessarily austere. For — and this is very dangerous — it binds the consciences with fetters tighter than they were bound by the word of God.

Calvin insists that life is a *peregrinatio,* and he urges that one should make good use of it and not indulge in excesses. One should — he says, using a phrase characteristic of that era of reawakened spirituality — use things as if one was not attached to them. [62] This is the only external limitation which Calvin

---

[61] Jean Calvin, *Institutio Christianae Religionis* (London, 1576), Bk. III, Ch. 10.

[62] This Pauline notion also occurs in *Don Quijote* where Cide Hamete cites it as one of the characteristic features of the Christian religion:

Yo, aunque moro, bien sé, por la comunicación que he tenido con cristianos, que la santidad consiste en la caridad, humildad, fee, obediencia y pobreza; pero, con todo eso, digo que ha de tener mucho de Dios el que se viniere a contentar con ser pobre,

imposes. He disavows any more strenuous privations, rejecting as useless and misguided the efforts of monks and ascetics to achieve salvation through privation and chastisement of the body. Calvin thus rejects this active form of *peregrinatio*, because it was not prescribed by the Bible. Because of this he rejects all manifestations of this type of *peregrinatio*: asceticism, devotionary pilgrimages, and Purgatory. For him only the Biblical *peregrinatio* has validity.

The reaction of other Protestants was either equal or analogous to that of Calvin and it is reflected in literature. One of the most renowned Protestant books treating the *peregrinatio vitae* theme is John Bunyan's *The Pilgrim's Progress* (1678). Here the problem of the manner of salvation is raised in the first paragraph by Christian who, reading about the imminent destruction of his city, calls out despairingly: "What shall I do [to be saved]?" He is then directed to go to the Celestial City, which he reaches after traversing many trying obstacles in the course of his pilgrimage.

> si no es de aquel modo de pobreza de quien dice uno de sus mayores santos: "Tened todas las cosas como si no las tuviésedes" (II, 44).
>
> Although I am a moor I know well from my acquaintance with Christians that saintliness consists of charity, humility, faith, obedience and poverty. Nevertheless, I maintain that someone who would content himself with poverty must have a great deal of God in him, unless it is the kind of poverty of which one of the greatest saints comments: "Possess all things as though you did not possess them."

Leo Spitzer once remarked that this admonition to detach oneself from the things of this world was a characteristic feature of baroque ideology, especially in Spain:

> Perhaps there is no "baroque man"; what there is is a baroque attitude, which is, in short, a fundamentally Christian attitude: "to possess as if one did not possess" *(tener como si no se tuviera)*.

(Translated from "El barroco español," *Romanische Literaturstudien* [Tübingen, 1959], p. 801). One might add that this was true not only in Catholic Spain but, as Calvin testifies, that it held true with respect to Protestants and Catholics alike, that therefore it is perhaps indicative of the religious revival which swept Europe in general during the sixteenth century. The fervor of both Reformation and Counter Reformation was the result of that revival.

Calvin states that the idea of detachment is a fundamental attribute of the *peregrinatio vitae*. We might conclude therefore that it was the combination of these ideas that shaped the baroque outlook on the world.

A comparison with Dante's *peregrinatio* in the *Divina Com-media* would at this point seem rather tempting. We note, however, that the journey of Dante and his fellow penitents is a purgatorial one; it illustrates therefore the principle of salvation through works. This principle is, however, emphatically rejected in *The Pilgrim's Progress:* "For a man can receive nothing except it be given him from Heaven; all is Grace, not of works" (p. 77). Christian's journey then is not a purgatorial *peregrinatio;* it is a purely Biblical *peregrinatio vitae:*

> The men [i.e., Christian and his Companion] told them that they were Pilgrims and Strangers in the world and that they were going to their own Country, which was the Heavenly Jerusalem (p. 90).

Unlike the hardships of Dante, those of Christian are not there to purify him of his sins but merely serve as obstacles, symbolic of those which occur in life. Christian reaches Paradise not because he has suffered meritoriously but because he has persisted in his faith. He saves himself not through works but through faith.

The Roman Catholic Concept of PEREGRINATIO VITAE

Nevertheless, while Protestants doubted the individual's capacity to work for his own salvation, Catholics not only affirmed it but in the Council of Trent emphatically reasserted it. This meant that, as before, the passive Biblical *peregrinatio* could be turned into an active, ascetic one. This is perhaps most strikingly illustrated by the literary figure of the *pícaro.*

Originally, as in *Lazarillo de Tormes* (1554), the *pícaro* was conceived as an impoverished youth who, living alone and on the edge of starvation, attempts to make a living by fair means or foul, shunning only homicide. His only concern is his physical survival; anything beyond that, any "meta-physical" considerations, do not enter his mind. This characterization changes somewhat in a continuation of the *Lazarillo* written by Juan de Luna (1620) where Lázaro is more inclined to make abstract consideration about his life:

Tendido en la puerta de la iglesia y haciendo alarde de mi vida pasada, consideraba los infortunios en que me había visto desde el día que comencé a servir al ciego hasta el punto en que me hallaba. [63]

As I was lying at the church door, reviewing my past life, I considered the misfortunes in which I had seen myself since the day I began to serve the blind man until the present.

A sympathetic hermit lends an ear to his lamentations:

Como el buen padre me vio afligido, con palabras dulces y blandas me comenzó a consolar, preguntándome de dónde era, y qué sucesos me habían traído a tal término. Contéle con breves y sucintas razones el largo proceso de mi amarga peregrinación; quedó admirado de oírme, y con piedad y lástima que mostró tener de mí, me convidó con su ermita (p. 125b).

When the good father saw me suffering he began to console me with sweet and soft words, asking me where I was from, and what events had brought me to such a condition. I told him in brief and succinct words the long process of my bitter journey. He was astonished at what he heard, and showing me great commiseration and pity he invited me into his hermitage.

Lázaro sizes up his vagabond life as a painful *peregrinación,* admitting that his life has been consumed by unsuccessful attempts to improve his lot. He is even inclined to become a hermit himself. But before he can put his resolution into effect the hermit dies, and Lázaro's good intentions are usurped by his avaricious preoccupation to inherit the belongings of the deceased. As a result his ambition to be a hermit degenerates into a mere expedient for worldly aims, which, not surprisingly, plunge him into even greater worldly misfortunes. In the end after many persecutions and beatings he seeks refuge in a church and awaits death.

Luna's *Lazarillo* thus ends with the *pícaro* in a state of frustration and despair, a far cry from the Lázaro of the first

---

[63] *BAE,* III, 125b. In this edition the author's name appears as H. de Luna.

part who settles down, smugly content with his newly acquired, modest station. The second Lázaro is aware of the futility of the picaresque struggle for existence; he looks back on a life misspent. This awareness appears even more acutely in Mateo Alemán's novel *Vida de Guzmán de Alfarache* (1599). Its protagonist roams through Spain and Italy; he serves many men; he cheats and is cheated, often manhandled, until he is condemned to the galleys for robbery. He too characterizes his wandering pursuit as a *peregrinatio:*

> salí a ver mundo, peregrinando por él, encomendándome a Dios y buenas gentes en quien hice confianzas. [64]

> I left to see the world, wandering about in it, commending myself to God and the good people in whom I confided.

Wandering is a fundamental aspect of the picaresque life and so are hardships and frustrations. In addition to that it is fraught with innumerable moral pitfalls into which the *pícaro* plunges most readily. In short, the picaresque life mirrors the condition of the *peregrinatio vitae* in its most aggravated form.

Not surprisingly Guzmán too is overcome by the awareness of having wasted his life:

> Rematé la cuenta con mi mala vida. La que después gasté todo el restante della verás en la tercera y última parte, si el cielo me la diere antes de la eterna que todos esperamos. [65]

> I closed the account with my evil life. The remainder of which I wasted, as you shall see in the third and last part, if Heaven should grant it to me, before [granting me] the eternal [life] to which we all look forward.

This statement, made by Guzmán the narrator at an advanced age, shows how vastly his sense of morality has improved since

---

[64] *La vida de Guzmán de Alfarache,* ed. Samuel Gili y Gaya, in *Clásicos Castellanos,* Part I, Ch. 2.
[65] *Guzmán de Alfarache,* III, 9.

the time of his youthful exploits. One suspects that somewhere in the course of that time he experienced a radical conversion, that he returned to the path of virtue by making use of that option open to every true Catholic, the road of active penitence. In terms of the logic of his spiritual progress, then, Guzmán's narrative is incomplete. Presumably Alemán would have presented that spiritual turnabout in his promised third part.

The third part never appeared. Nevertheless the *Guzmán* was a highly popular work and in its own time achieved more editions than *Don Quijote*. In Golden-Age Spain a popular book would often provoke spurious imitators to write continuations, and the *Guzmán* was no exception. The most famous of these continuations was published in 1603 by Mateo Luxán de Sayavedra (pseudonym for Juan Martí). And in the 1640's another one was written by one Machado de Silva, which begins its narration with Guzmán's release from the galleys. A letter from his mother informs him that he is in fact the son of a nobleman. This news affects Guzmán profoundly; the consciousness of his nobility suddenly makes him aware of the depravity of his former life:

> Gran freno deve de ser la nobleza de acciones infames, porque al mismo tiempo que entendí ser hijo deste último padre, tan horrendas se me representaron las picardías de mi vida, que si es posible fuera a bolver a deshazerlas con ofrecerme a los mayores trabajos. [66]

> Nobility must be a strong brake to infamous actions, because as soon as I learned that I was the son of this latter father, the rogueries of my life appeared to me so horrifying, that, had it been possible, I would have turned back to undo them by offering myself to the greatest hardships.

So strong is his loathing of his vices that he would willingly submit to arduous penitence. This opportunity does, in fact, arise. He recalls that in a moment of danger he had vowed to do a pilgrimage:

---

[66] Félix Machado de Silva, *"Tercera parte de Guzmán de Alfarache,"* ed. Gerhard Moldenhauer, *RH*, LXIX (1927), 36. The novel remained unpublished until this edition appeared.

> dixe que era forzoso partirme el siguiente día a Santiago de Galizia, vestido de peregrino, por voto que en un peligro grande, de que él me sacara, avía hecho (p. 43).

> I said that I had to leave the next day to go to Santiago in Galicia, dressed as a pilgrim, to fulfill a vow I had made when he [Santiago] had retrieved me from a great peril.

Now he has greater reason than ever to accomplish it and he does so wholeheartedly. In this way he turns the aimless, depraved *peregrinatio* of picaresque life into a directed, devotional *peregrinatio,* striving thereby to undo his past sins and to renew his chances for salvation.

This spiritual turnabout was very much in keeping with the philosophy of the Counter Reformation, and not surprisingly it recurs in other picaresque works. A German translator of Alemán's *Guzmán,* Aeguidius Albertinus (1560-1620), produced his own continuation to Alemán's version. In it Guzmán likewise undertakes a pilgrimage to atone for his sinful life, this time to the Holy Land. [67] And the most renowned German imitation of the picaresque genre, Grimmelshausen's *Simplicius Simplicissimus* (1669), also makes use of this feature.

Simplicius flees his native farm as a boy, when it is sacked by roving soldiers. In a country torn by the ravages of the Thirty-Years War he then proceeds to make a living. Initially without guile, he faces the cruel world with that sincere simplicity which his name indicates. With his innate intelligence, however, he learns to cope skilfully with his environment, to deceive and to cheat while roaming about the countryside. But success and tranquility never come to him, and disillusioned at last with the world he retreats to a hermitage:

> Behüte dich Gott, Welt, dann mich verdreust deine Conversation. Das Leben, so du uns gibest, ist eine elende Pilgerfahrt, ein unbeständiges, ungewisses, hartes, rauhes, hinflüchtiges und unreines Leben voll Armseeligkeit und

---

[67] See Franz Rauhut, "La picaresca española en la literatura alemana," *RFH,* I (1939), 247.

Irrtum, welches vielmehr ein Tod als ein Leben zu nen-
nen; in welchem wir alle Augenblicke sterben durch viel
Gebrechen der Unbeständigkeit und durch mancherley
Wege des Todes. [68]

Godspeed to you, world, for your company annoys me.
That life which you give us is a miserable pilgrimage, an
unstable, uncertain, difficult, rough, fleeting and impure
life, full of weakness and error, which ought rather to be
called death than life; in which we are dying at every
moment of the infirmities of instability, and of the various
approaches of death.

For Simplicius, then, life is a miserable *Pilgerfahrt,* a *peregrinatio
vitae* at its worst. He, the *picaro,* experienced it in its most aggravated form, and he draws his lesson from it. From now on he
refuses to participate any longer in the senseless struggle.

With the pessimistic note the original version of *Simplicissimus*
ends. But the wide acclaim of the book prompted Grimmelshausen
to write a sequel which begins its portrayal of the protagonist by
showing him meditating, among other things, on the life of
St. Alexis:

Das Leben des heiligen Alexi kam mir im ersten Griff
unter die Augen, als ich das Buch aufschlug, da fand ich,
mit was vor einer Vorachtung der Ruhe er das reiche
Hauss seines Vatters verlassen, die heiligen Oerter hin
und wieder mit grosser Andacht besuchet und endlich
beydes seine Pilgerschaft und Leben unter einer Stiegen
in höchster Armuth, mit unvergleichlicher Geduld und
wunderbarer Beständigkeit seeliglich beschlossen hatte
(VI, 10).

At first glance I happened to set my eyes on the *Life
of St. Alexis,* and when I opened the book I found out
with how much disregard to comfort he had left the
wealthy home of his father, and with great piety visited
the holy places, and had finally happily concluded both
his pilgrimage and his life under a stairway in utmost
poverty, unequaled patience and wonderful steadfastness.

---

[68] Johann Jakob Christoffel von Grimmelshausen, *Der abentheuerliche
Simplicius Simplicissimus,* ed. Felix Bobertag (Berlin, 1882-83), Book V,
Ch. 24.

He notes that St. Alexis lived in a state of *Pilgerschaft*, that is, an active ascetic *peregrinatio*, under the stairs of his father's house. In view of this Simplicius criticizes himself for not being active and showing his devotion in an active way:

> Ach! sagte ich zu mir selbst, Simplici, was thust du? du liegst hier auf der faulen Bärenhaut und dienest weder Gott noch Menschen! wer allein ist, wann derselbe fallet, wer wird ihm wieder aufhelffen? ist es nicht besser, du dienest deinem Neben-Menschen und sie dir hingegen hinwiederum als dass du hier ohn alle Leutseeligkeit in der Einsame sitzest wie eine Nacht-Eule? (VI, 10).

> Oh, Simplicius, I said to myself, what are you doing? Here you are lying about and serve neither God nor man. When one is alone who will help him? Would it not be better if you helped neighbor, so that he might in turn help you, instead of remaining in this solitude like a night owl!

His deliberation results in a desire to become active by making a pilgrimage to the Holy Land:

> Mit solchen und dergleichen Anfechtungen und Gedanken ward ich gequälet, biss ich mich endlich entschloss, aus einem Wald- ein Wallbruder oder Pilger zu werden (VI, 10).

> With such [internal] conflicts and thoughts I was tormented until I finally decided to change from a forest-dweller into a pilgrim.

Simplicius, like Guzmán, thus translates an aimless *peregrinatio* into an active, meritorious one, thereby turning disillusionment at the world into hope for eternal life.

Thus both the *Simplicissimus* and the *Guzmán* illustrate the degree to which the picaresque novel was adaptable to the ideals of the Counter Reformation. They portray within the complex concept of *peregrinatio* what official Catholicism held most dear: the spectacle of the returning truant, who by his own free will [69]

---

[69] A. A. Parker stresses the important function of free will in the picaresque novel: "First, man is free to choose between good and evil; there is

mends his ways and repents by performing works of piety. The *pícaro* is the arch-truant of baroque literature. If an individual of his baseness was able to find grace, then certainly the average man could too. The picaresque novel thus lent itself as a potentially unique vehicle for demonstrating the workings of the faith.

The PEREGRINATIO of Worldly Reconnaissance

This adaptability testifies to what extent the concept of the picaresque novel has broadened since *Lazarillo de Tormes*. The latter is in a sense still basically a dramatized treatise on survival techniques. Survival, of course, continues to be the *pícaro*'s prominent motive in later novels such as Quevedo's *El buscón*. But it is no longer the exclusive motive. In the Guzmán-versions and in the *Simplicissimus* the picaresque genre shows its ability to expand into a spectacle of truancy and recantation. In fact, even in Alemán's *Guzmán* survival is rather a secondary concern. The protagonist does not leave home to make a living. Belonging to a middle-class family, he is actually well off. Rather what compels him to leave is his desire to escape the unbearable moral climate at home and his longing to see the world:

> El mejor medio que hallé fue probar la mano para salir de miseria, dejando mi madre y tierra. Hícelo así; y para no ser conocido no me quise valer del apellido de mi padre; púseme el Guzmán de mi madre y Alfarache de la heredad adonde tuve mi principio. Con esto salí a ver mundo, peregrinando por él, encomendándome a Dios y buenas gentes en quien hice confianza. [70]

---

no determinism; ... man can therefore of his own free will cooperate with Divine Grace to make his salvation effective." (*Literature and the Delinquent* [Edinburgh, 1967], p. 39.) To experience and utilize this spiritual freedom, to test his choice of good and evil in action, the *pícaro* needs freedom of action, which is the hallmark of his genre: "The picaresque novel thus arises as an exposition of the theme of freedom, including the concept of moral freedom" (p. 19).

[70] Alemán, *Guzmán*, Pt. I, Ch. 2. The suppression of the survival motive is especially evident in Cervantes' exemplary novel *La ilustre fregona*. Here Diego de Carriazo, the son of an upper-class family, leaves home for the pure joy of experiencing the picaresque life:

> Trece años, o poco más, tendría Carriazo, cuando, llevado de una inclinación picaresca, sin forzarle a ello ningún mal tratamiento

The best way [of attaining relief] that I could find
was to try my hand at escaping from misery, by leaving
my mother and my homeland. So I did; and in order not
to be recognized I avoided using the surname of my
father. I named myself Guzmán after my mother and
Alfarache after the heritage from which I originated. With
this I left to see the world, wandering about in it, com-
mending myself to God and the good people in whom I
confided.

For Guzmán, then, the desire to explore the world is at least as
strong a motive for leaving home as is the domestic depravity. His
peregrinatio is therefore one of reconnaissance of the world; he
becomes a roving observer, moving from object to object, later
to evaluate his experience critically as a narrator in a mature age.

---

que sus padres le hiciesen, sólo por su gusto y antojo, desgarró,
como dicen los muchachos, de casa de sus padres, y se fue por
ese mundo adelante, tan contento de la vida libre, que en la mitad
de las incomodidades y miserias que trae consigo no echaba menos
la abundancia de la casa de su padre. . . .

Carriazo must have been about thirteen years old when he was
gripped by a picaresque yearning, and even though no mistreatment
by his parents forced him to do it, he eloped, as they say, from his
parents' house out of pure enjoyment and desire. And he made
his way through the world, so delighted with his free life that in
the midst of the inevitable discomforts and miseries he did not
miss the abundance of his father's house. . . .

(Cited from *Las novelas ejemplares,* ed. Francisco Rodríguez Marín, in
Clásicos Castellanos XXVII, 221-222.) To hide his noble ascendency he
changes his name:

Es de advertir que en su peregrinación don Diego mudó el nombre de Carriazo en el de Urdiales, y con este nombre se hizo llamar
de los que el suyo no sabían (p. 229).

It must be noted that in his wanderings don Diego changed his
name Carriazo to Urdiales, and he let himself be called by
that name by those who did not know his real one.

Diego's need to change his name underlines the fact that he does not
belong in the picaresque world. For him the picaresque life is just a role
which he takes up for only a temporary period. Like an actor he temporarily
changes his identity for this role and changes it back again when his
performance is over. Nothing could be further from the motive of survival,
which compels the individual to commit himself to the picaresque life un-
reservedly and for an undetermined amount of time. Diego's motive then
is primarily the desire to explore the picaresque life. His *peregrinatio* is
one of reconnaissance, designed to satisfy his craving for the picaresque
experience.

Evidently such a *peregrinatio* of reconnaissance appealed to the contemporary reader, because it appears in a host of other prose works of that time. The reader delighted in the accounts of the experience of ever-new variety, of new and surprising encounters of a protagonist wandering through the world, and his reactions to it. Gracián in *El discreto* tells why this is so:

> Empleó el segundo en peregrinar, que fue gustoso peregrino; segunda felicidad para un hombre de curiosidad y buena nota. Buscó y gozó de todo lo bueno y lo mejor del mundo; que quien no ve las cosas no goza enteramente de ellas: va mucho de lo visto a lo imaginado: mas gusta de los objetos el que los ve una vez que el que muchas; porque aquélla se gozan y los demás enfadan. . . . Adquiérese aquella ciencia experimental, tan estimada de los sabios, especialmente cuando el que registra atiende y sabe reparar, examinándolo todo o con admiración o con desengaño. [71]

> The second one took to wandering; he was a contented wanderer. This is the second happiness for a man of curiosity and good standing. He searched out and enjoyed all the good and the best which the world had to offer him. For he who does not see things does not enjoy them completely. There is a great distinction between seeing and imagining. He who sees things once enjoys them more than he who [sees] them many times, because that [one time] can be enjoyed whereas the others annoy. . . . This experimental knowledge, so esteemed by wise men, is especially [well] acquired when he who surveys [these things] pays heed and knows how to observe by examining everything with either wonderment or disillusionment.

According to Gracián, one enjoys an object most when one is in its presence, if one sees it. Experience can reveal best the true nature of the object. It is not enough to imagine it, for the imagination cannot be trusted.

One senses in this attitude a touch of neurosis. Man feels constantly compelled to examine reality over and over again, never quite satisfied with the results of his observations. As a

---

[71] Cited from Vilanova, "El peregrino andante," p. 155.

consequence man feels less secure of his environment. The extent to which this insecurity may go is illustrated by Cervantes' *Don Quijote*. To Don Quijote things and objects never really "are," they only "seem to be." Truth is elusive and verifiable only through repeated checking, "para sacar una verdad en limpio menester son muchas pruebas y repruebas" (II, 26). Throughout *Don Quijote*, therefore, the search for authentic proof never ceases, as evidenced by such expressions as "ver con los ojos" and "tocar con al mano" which by their very redundancy underline the obsessive need for verification. Only by approaching the object as closely as possible, preferably within seeing and touching distance, can one hope to explore its real nature.

What holds true with respect to individual objects also pertains to the world as a whole. To learn about the world, to experience the variety of creation, one must go near each object, and examine it, then proceed to the next one, thus wandering in a perpetual *peregrinatio* of discovery. We have already seen how the voyages of discovery were designated by the concept of *peregrinatio*. [72] These voyages produced encounters with unknown worlds, thereby rendering the traditional Ptolemaic image of the world inadequate. Knowledge gained from observation thus proved to be more pertinent than preconceived ideas, the truth of experience more powerful than the truth of precept.

It is not surprising, therefore, that the belief in the validity of experience and in the process of discovery should become a state of mind which was carried from one field of endeavor to another, from the field of geographic discovery into the field of philosophy and literature. In Gracián's work *El criticón* (1651), the *peregrinatio* of discovery is, as we have seen, directly linked with the *peregrinatio vitae*. Life, like a voyage of discovery, is full of surprising encounters:

> Varias y grandes son las monstruosidades que se van descubriendo de nuevo cada día en la arriesgada peregrinación de la vida humana. Entre todas, la más portentosa es el estar del Engaño en la entrada del mundo y el

---

[72] See our Chapter I.

Desengaño a la salida, inconveniente tan perjudicial que basta a echar a perder todo el vivir.... [73]

Various and great are the monstrosities which one re-discovers every day in the dangerous pilgrimage of human life. The greatest among them is the appearance of Deception at the world's entrance and of Disillusionment at the exit, an obstacle so harmful that it suffices to spoil all of life. ...

The *peregrinatio vitae*, then, consists of a process of moral exploration of the world whose ultimate purpose is the attainment of *desengaño*, a wisdom of disillusionment. For Gracián the attainment of this wisdom is a necessary constituent of true virtue. Virtue itself is therefore in part a result of discovery. [74]

The literary genre which most blatantly thrives on the surprise encounter is the Milesian romance. The dizzying rapidity with which the characters are driven from one locale to another, and the frequency of their chance encounters may strike the modern reader as arbitrarily contrived. His sixteenth- and seventeenth-century counterpart, however, found this feature appealing because it struck a chord in him. It brought to his mind an intense awareness of the ever-changing, unstable condition of the *peregrinatio vitae*. Proof of this enthusiasm is the fact that two such illustrious writers as Lope and Cervantes should feel obliged

---

[73] Gracián, *El criticón*, Pt. III, Ch. 5.

[74] Therefore the search for, and attainment of, virtue depends on the individual's own effort. It is not handed to him ready-made in the form of historical models to be imitated effortlessly. This approach to moralism gives Gracián an exceptional place among Spanish moralists of his time:

> Unlike Quevedo or Saavedra Fajardo, Gracián holds up no model of noble virtues for the reader to imitate. If one would live the good life in society, no exemplar resurrected from history can serve as well as diligent exercise of self-criticism and self-control. To illuminate his point, Gracián, in the *Criticón*, dramatizes a broad range of temptations, challenges and uncertainties, to which the reader can respond — thoughtlessly like Andrenio, or judiciously like Critilo. Instead of indoctrination, this allegorical voyage through life attempts to shape judgments, and therefore represents a different approach to moral instruction.

See Monroe Z. Hafter, *Gracián and Perfection: Spanish Moralists of the Seventeenth Century* (Cambridge, Mass., 1966), p. 169.

to produce rival imitations, *El peregrino en su patria* and *Persiles y Sigismunda,* respectively. In both works the theme of the. *peregrinatio vitae* is a dominant one, and the hazards and dangers to which the characters are exposed are continuously cited as being illustrative of the whole of the human condition. The exaggeration of these hazards could only enhance the demonstrative quality of these works. In a sense they had the value of a laboratory wherein the principle of *peregrinatio* was reenacted. The conditions in a laboratory situation are of necessity contrived, but not because of this are the experiments less valid. Besides, who dare assert that events in real life may not outdo the laboratory results?

PEREGRINATIO *and Narrative Form*

The intricacy and multiplicity of the events in the Milesian tale also posed a problem for the author. Cervantes in his *Persiles* stresses the difficulty of managing the narrative complexity:

> Las peregrinaciones largas siempre traen consigo diversos acontecimientos; y como la diversidad se compone de cosas diferentes es forçoso que los casos lo sean. Bien nos lo muestra esta historia, cuyos acontecimientos nos cortan su hilo, poniéndonos en duda dónde será bien anudarle. ...[75]

> Long journeys always bring with them diverse events; and since diversity is composed of different things, the events, too, are different. This is well demonstrated by our story, whose divers events cause us to lose the narrative thread, putting us in doubt where to retie it. ...

Cervantes complains that the diversity and variety of experience which the *peregrinatio* entails prevents proper organization of the story. At worst the narrative will be as erratic and as fraught with interruptions as the *peregrinatio* itself. Not without justification, therefore, Cervantes dubs his work a *peregrina historia.* [76] Here the

---

[75] *Persiles y Sigismunda,* Pt. III, Ch. 10.

[76] II, 21. A structural equivalence of the subject matter to the narration is also emphasized in *Don Quijote* by Fernando in his evaluation of the Cautivo's story:

adjective *peregrino* describes primarily the strange, uncommon, baffling events which the story relates; but it also carries an overtone of the wandering, erratic quality of the narrative. The path of the story tries to follow and adjust itself to the path of the characters' *peregrinatio*; the narrative itself thus becomes a microcosm, a mirror image, of the events in the story. The concept *peregrina historia* might therefore appropriately describe other baroque prose works dealing with the theme of *peregrinatio*, such as the picaresque novel and Cervantes' own *Don Quijote*, [77] works in which the unforeseen encounters are legion, in which characters

---

> Por cierto, señor capitán, el modo con que habéis contado este extraño suceso ha sido tal, que iguala a la novedad y extrañeza del mesmo caso. Todo es peregrino, y raro, y lleno de accidentes que maravillan y suspenden a quien las oye: ... (I, 42).

> Certainly, Captain, your way of reporting this strange event has been such that it matches the novelty and strangeness of the case itself. Everything is strange, odd, and full of occurrences which astonish and stupefy anyone who hears of them. ...

The manner of narration, Fernando observes, reflects the *peregrino y raro* quality, the strangeness of the adventures. At the same time, too, the adjective *peregrino* includes an overtone of the Cautivo's wandering. It is, after all, in the course of his errant adventure that he makes his strange encounters. In his attempt to be as accurate as possible, he adjusts his narrative to the changing trail of the events. This, he admits, is a problematic undertaking, because it tempts him to ramble:

> No tengo más, señores, que deciros de mi historia; la cual, si es agradable y peregrina, júzguenlo vuestros buenos entendimientos; que de mi sé decir que quisiera habérosla contado más brevemente, puesto que el temor de enfadaros más de cuatro circunstancias me ha quitado de la lengua (I, 41).

> I have nothing more to tell you of my story, gentlemen. Whether it is agreeable or strange, let your sound minds judge. I can only say that I would have liked to tell it to you in briefer fashion; in fact, the fear of annoying you has already made me omit at least four incidents.

[77] We note in the following passage that the term *peregrina historia* is also applied to the wanderings of Don Quijote himself. Here the canon listens to the priest's account of the knight's adventures:

> ... estuvo atento a todo aquello que decirle quiso de la condición, vida, locura y costumbres de Don Quijote, contándole brevemente el principio y causa de su desvarío, y todo el progreso de sus sucesos, hasta haberlo puesto en aquella jaula, y el disignio que llevaban de llevarle a su tierra, para ver si por algun medio hallaban remedio a su locura. Admiráronse de nuevo los criados y el canónigo de oír la peregrina historia de Don Quijote, ... (I, 47).

are confronted with forever new and startling aspects of reality
in a continuous process of reconnaissance.

We have already dealt with another instance wherein the theme
of *peregrinatio* characterized a literary form, namely the verses of
Las soledades which Góngora described as *pasos de un peregrino.* [78] The form of the verses is the *silva* whose irregular lines
are highly suitable to describe the erratic excursion of the shipwrecked youth into the strange pastoral world. As the *peregrino*-lover gropes his way through the unknown land, so the
peregrino-poet, whose steps are the verses, explore the no-man's-
land of a new concept of poetry. Here, too, the style, the choice
of the medium, reflect the subject matter. There is, furthermore,
evidence in the poem of an additional third type of *peregrinatio*,
a *peregrinatio vitae*. The poem was designed to comprise the four
seasons which in contemporary thought frequently signify the
four divisions of human life, which are moreover related to
the *peregrinatio vitae*. [79] The wanderings of the youth thus have
a representative quality: they symbolize the errant course of
human life. This hypothesis is strengthened by the fact that in

---

Here again the implications of the term are complex. It refers on the one
hand to the startling strangeness which the newcomers perceive in the mad
exploits of Don Quijote. But Don Quijote's case history also includes the
"progreso de sus sucesos," that is, his adventures are seen as a consecutive
sequence of separate experiences which, like beads on a string, correspond
to the errant trail of his *peregrinatio*. The term *peregrina historia* echoes
this sequence. Don Quijote, then, is engaged on a *peregrinatio* of exploration,
whose outstanding feature is that it is carried out by a madman. Madness
resembles the condition of *peregrinatio* in that the individual views the
world from the abnormal vantage point of an outsider. The experiences
and observations of a madman may therefore be as illuminating as that
of a *peregrinus*. It seems appropriate, therefore, that the baroque period,
which makes such overwhelming use of the concept of *peregrinatio,* should
also find mental estrangement to be such a fascinating subject matter for
literary treatment.

[78] See our Chapter I.

[79] Gracián divides *El criticón* into three parts which encompass the
four seasons in the following manner:

> Primera Parte: En la primavera de la niñez y en el estío de la
> juventud. Segunda Parte: En el otoño de la edad varonil. Tercera
> Parte: En el invierno de la vejez.
> First Part: In the Springtime of Childhood and the Summer of
> Youth. Second Part: In the Autumn of Manhood. Third Part: In
> the Winter of Old Age.

Góngora's poem the youth is not named and instead only circumscribed by the general epithet *el peregrino*. As in the *peregrina historia* the concept of *peregrinatio* spans a whole spectrum of meanings: the concepts of the style, of the plot and of life itself are woven into one conceptual whole, testifying thereby to the extent to which the idea of *peregrinatio* permeated the thought process of the writer, and, in fact, of an entire era.

Both the *peregrina historia* and the *peregrino*-verses signalize a high point in the development of the metaphor. They are the ultimate evidence of the complex constellation of meanings to which the original Biblical *peregrinatio* gave rise. The development started when the early Christians fashioned out of the Biblical *peregrinatio vitae* a second applied concept, a prescription for a meritorious life actively pursued. By doing so they initiated a powerful tradition of institutions such as monasticism, the pilgrimage, the holy war and Purgatory, most of which remain valid for a large part of Christianity. Protestants disavowed most of that tradition and retained only the Biblical idea that fathered it. Catholics, however, retained it and during the baroque era both camps revitalized the consciousness of the idea, each according to its own beliefs. This renewal resulted largely from the man's growing awareness in the sixteenth century that his universe had begun to change rapidly. Disturbed by a feeling of insecurity he took increased refuge in faith. In the writings and institutions of his faith he found a concept which adequately summed up his plight: the concept of *peregrinatio vitae*. At the same time, while this concept defined his condition, it also spelled consolation for him, because he knew that the *peregrinatio*'s proper destination was Paradise. Thus in the midst of an unstable world this concept provided him with the hope and the vision of restful stability somewhere apart from the earthly turmoil.

CONCLUSION

The outstanding feature of the concept of *peregrinatio* in the baroque age is the Christian character which it had developed over a period of a millenium and a half. Christ himself embodied the status of the *peregrinus*, and because of this Divine precedent Christianity came to champion the cause of the human *peregrinus*: in the person of the ascetic saint it made him the object of veneration. Christianity thus became the religion of the stranger, of the outsider who has little stake in this temporal world. For the pagan, life on earth was the end-all of his thinking and endeavor. Christianity changed this outlook. It produced the vision of a more perfect existence, of an afterlife in Paradise compared to which earthly life was pure hardship and drudgery. In Paradise there was stability, whereas life on earth was uncertain and unstable. The temporal life had, in short, all the properties of the *peregrinatio*. Compared to the pagan concept of life, this new understanding meant in effect a devaluation of earthly life. The Christian, in taking it less for granted, did not feel at home in it.

The idea of instability and hardship which the Christian *peregrinatio* implied became a habit of mind which was carried over into other realms of thought. In particular it found its application in the literary portrayal of love. The troubadours established the hypothesis that mental anguish with respect to love offered a far more memorable and significant experience than the simple satisfaction conferred by requital and consummation. This recognition produced a psychological sophistication unmatched by any precedents in pagan antiquity. Without the mental conditioning which the troubadour received from his Christian education it is unlikely that he would have been able to acquire such subtle insights into the human psyche. The gaining of insights into the interior of man is a fundamental endeavor of Christian theologians. Seen in this light, a large part of the corpus of patristic literature represents a gigantic, elaborate attempt to cope with the complexity of the human soul.

By its very nature, then, the heightened consciousness of the Christian *peregrinatio* turns man's gaze inward, because he has detached himself from those worldly things with which, as a stranger, he has little need to involve himself. In the baroque age the necessity of gazing inwardly was given a new emphasis, which represents in large part a reaction to the extroversion of the preceding period of the Renaissance. The humanistic revival of learning had turned man's attention to the exterior world. His exultation over its discovery was epitomized in the writings of Rabelais. Because the *peregrinatio* of Pantagruel was exclusively directed to the exploration of the plenitude of the temporal world, it bore little resemblance to the spiritual *peregrinatio* of Christianity. Since, however, the decrees of the Council of Trent imposed a new seriousness on Catholic intellectual life, it is this spiritual *peregrinatio* that prevailed in the age of the baroque.

The fact that the literary theme of the spiritual *peregrinatio* requires a great capacity for introspection is borne out by its high incidence in the soul-searching literature of Romanticism. We cannot, within the scope of this exposition, do more than suggest the literary fortunes of *peregrinatio* after the baroque age. But it is necessary for the reader not to lose sight of the continuing nature of the tradition. It is true that, because the Enlightenment generally avoided religious metaphors, our theme remained in a comparatively latent state during the eighteenth century. But with the advent of Romanticism it burst anew on the imaginative consciousness of poets. A pair of illustrations must suffice.

In *Childe Harold's Pilgrimage* (1818) Lord Byron treats the theme of *peregrinatio* under the guise of a youth of noble birth who suddenly feels a severe discontent as a result of his life of plenty and comfort in the parental home. To compensate, he seeks the experience of hardships incurred by wandering in distant lands: "With pleasure drugg'd, he almost longed for woe." [1] In the same way that the cause of his change of spirit is inexplicable, so the goal of his *peregrinatio* is undefined:

> Onward he flies, nor fix'd as yet the goal
> Where he shall rest him on his pilgrimage;
> And o'er him many changing scenes must roll
> Ere toil his thirst for travel can assuage,
> Or he shall calm his breast, or learn experience sage (I, 28).

Harold's pilgrimage, then, is a flight away from worldly stability and ease. In its form it resembles the meritorious *peregrinatio* implied in the early ascetic's emphatic renunciation of worldly comfort.

We find a similar renunciation in a poem by Schiller entitled *Der Pilgrim* (1803). Here too the youth renounced his rich inheritance to take up a life of wandering:

> Noch in meines Lebens Lenze
> War ich, und wandert aus,
> Und der Jugend frohe Tänze
> Liess ich in des Vaters Haus.
>
> All mein Erbteil, meine Habe
> Warf ich fröhlich glaubend hin.
> Und am leichten Pilgerstabe
> Zog ich fort mit Kindersinn. [2]

> I was still in the springtime of my life, and I emigrated; and I left the happy dances of youth in the house of my father.
> All my inheritance and possessions I threw away with happy conviction. And with the light pilgrim's staff in hand I went away with a child's motivation.

He undertakes this sacrifice because he is searching for a type of earthly paradise in which everything is eternal:

---

[1] George Gordon (Lord Byron), *Childe Harold's Pilgrimage*, in *The Poetical Works* (London, 1960), Canto I, stanza 6.

[2] Friedrich Schiller, "Der Pilgrim," *Gesammelte Werke*, ed. Curt Noch (Berlin, 1955), I, 447.

Denn das Irdische wird dorten
Himmlisch unvergänglich sein.

For the earthly things will attain a Heavenly permanence
up there.

In both Byron's and Schiller's poems the renunciation of the
world resembles the ascetic *Weltflucht,* the meritorious *peregrinatio* which is the hallmark of much Catholic thought. This
Romantic form of asceticism derives from the fact that Romantic
writers in general tended to exalt Roman Catholicism because of
the appeal which its ritual and its call to renunciation made to
them. [3] The Romantic longed for a *Weltflucht* because he de-
spised the world as he saw it and sought a better human condition.
Like the ascetic, he thought that hardships and renunciation could
help him attain such a state.

Byron's poem also includes the semblance of another type of
meritorious *peregrinatio,* the devotional pilgrimage. In Canto IV
the pilgrim visits Rome and says: "My Pilgrim's shrine is won"
(IV, 174). The pilgrim's primary purpose in coming to Rome,
however, is not to adore the shrine. Instead he comes to contemplate Rome as a remnant of that empire whose rise and fall
illustrate the rise and fall of human endeavor:

> Oh Rome! my country! city of the soul!
> The orphans of the heart must turn to thee,
> Lone mother of dead empires (IV, 78).

Here we note the difference between the Romantic pilgrim and
the normal Christian pilgrim, as presented in the baroque. If the
latter vowed to make a pilgrimage to Rome, he would complete
that vow only when he worshipped at the shrine of St. Peter. The

---

[3]   The general inclination of the Romantics toward the Catholic
faith did not originate in a historical-esthetic trend, but in the
religious conviction that God's infinity was revealed in earthly
things. The Church was the symbol of the last mystic communion
in faith — in it the infinite became religious experience and reality.
Romanticism was a religious movement from its beginning.

Translated from Fritz Martini, *Deutsche Literaturgeschichte* (Stuttgart, 1961),
p. 320.

motive of the Romantic pilgrim Byron is not the official Christian one, but a personal one, [4] unrelated to his religious life. It is the typical Romantic motive of contemplating the past. By the same token his *peregrinatio* of ascetic renunciation is not motivated by an impulse of Christian piety but by a very personal need to escape. [5]

The Romantic *peregrinatio* is, therefore, more properly to be called a "quest." The mainspring of the quest lies in the universal laws of individual psychology, which transcend any particular religious or cultural sphere. On the other hand, the *peregrinatio* is inseparably bound up with the Christian heritage of the West. Up until, and especially during, the baroque this Christian heritage was still a powerful law which compelled the individual to align his psychic motives with the official religion. This law acted upon everything the individual said and thought like an electric field, charging it with a potentially Christian meaning. Since the concept of *peregrinatio* moved within this field, it too was inexorably charged with religious overtones, which helped to endow it with the complexity of meaning which makes it such a tantalizing object of study. After the baroque this exterior religious influence vanished to a great extent. Its disappearance meant that the complex

---

[4] That Harold's pilgrimage is also Byron's personal one is admitted by the poet himself:

> With regard to the conduct of the last canto there will be found less of the pilgrim than in any of the preceding, and that little slightly, if at all, separated from the author speaking in his own person. The fact is that I have become weary of drawing a line which everyone seemed determined not to perceive: like the Chinese in Goldsmith's "Citizen of the World," whom nobody would believe to be a Chinese, it was in vain that I asserted, and imagined that I had drawn, a distinction between the author and the pilgrim; and the very anxiety to preserve this difference, and disappointment at finding it unavailing, so far crushed my efforts in the composition, that I determined to abandon it altogether — and have done so.

See *Works,* p. 226b.

[5] Bernard Blackstone, who analyzes the English Romantics' favorite theme of travel, questions Childe Harold's motives:

> An embarrassment of motives, with only one serious omission: the overtly religious quest is lacking — no true pilgrimage (Byron's title is a misnomer), no search for the Grail.

See *The Lost Travellers* (London, 1962), p. 7.

interplay of individual motivation and religious law had on the whole ceased to affect the concept of *peregrinatio*. By the beginning of Romanticism the spiritual life of the individual had been largely enfranchized. By the same token the concept of *peregrinatio* became a personalized concept, which it has retained until this day.

SELECTED BIBLIOGRAPHY

Primary Sources

Achilles Tatius. *Leucippe and Clitophonte,* ed. and trans. S. Gaselee. London and New York, 1917.

Aischylos. *Die Schutzsuchenden,* ed. Walter Kraus. Frankfurt, 1948.

Alemán, Mateo. *La vida de Guzmán de Alfarache,* ed. Samuel Gili y Gaya. *Clásicos Castellanos,* Vols. 73, 83, 90, 93, 114.

Alpern, Hymen and José Martel, eds. *Diez comedias del Siglo de Oro.* New York, 1939.

Apophthegmata Patrum. PG, LXV, 71-440.

Ariosto, Ludovico. *Orlando Furioso,* ed. Santorre Debenedetti and Cesare Segre. Bologna, 1960.

Audiau, Jean, ed. *Nouvelle Anthologie des troubadours.* Paris, 1928.

Augustine, St. *De civitate Dei. PL,* XLI.

――――. *Confessionum Libri* XIII, *PL,* XXXII, 659-868.

Backer, Louis, ed. *L'Extrème Orient au Moyen Age.* Paris, 1877.

Basil, St. *Sermo de renuntiatione saeculi. PG,* XXXI, 628-648.

Beaumont, Francis and John Fletcher. *The Works,* ed. Arnold Glover. V-VI. Cambridge, 1905.

Bembo, Pietro. *Prose e Rime,* ed. Carlo Dionisotti. Torino, 1960.

Boccaccio, Giovanni. *Il Filocolo,* ed. Salvatore Battaglia. Bari, 1938.

――――. *Opere Volgari.* VII-VIII. Firenze, 1828.

Bonaventure, St. *Itinéraire de L'esprit vers Dieu,* ed. with trans. Henry Duméry. Paris, 1960.

Bradford, William. *History of Plymouth Plantation, 1606-1646,* ed. W. T. Davis. New York, 1908.

Brome, Richard. *The Dramatic Works.* III. London, 1873.

Brooke, Arthur. *The Tragical History of Romeus and Juliett.* In *The Plays of Shakespeare.* XIV. London, 1793.

Browning, Elizabeth Barrett. *The Poetical Works.* IV. London, 1890.

Bunyan, John. *The Pilgrim's Progress.* Rev. ed. by Roger Sharrock of the second ed. by James Blanton Wharey. Oxford, 1960.

Byron, Lord (George Gordon). *The Poetical Works.* London, 1960.

Calderón de la Barca, Pedro. *El mayor encanto amor. BAE,* VII, 390-410.

――――. *Obras completas,* ed. A. Valbuena Prat. 3 vols. Madrid, 1952.

Calvin, Jean. *Institutio Christianae Religionis.* London, 1576.

Camões, Luis de. *Os Lusíadas,* ed. J. D. M. Ford. Cambridge, Mass., 1946.

Castro, Adolfo de, ed. *Poetas líricos de los siglos XVI y XVII. BAE,* XXXII, XLII.

Castro, Guillén de. *Las mocedades del Cid,* ed. Victor Said Amestio. *Clásicos Castellanos,* Vol. 15. Madrid, 1962.

Cervantes Saavedra, Miguel de. *Don Quijote de la Mancha,* ed. Martín de Riquer. Barcelona, 1944.

————. *La Galatea,* ed. Juan B. Avalle-Arce. *Clásicos Castellanos,* Vols. 154, 155. Madrid, 1961.

————. *Novelas ejemplares,* ed. Francisco Rodríguez Marín. *Clásicos Castellanos,* Vols. 27, 36. Madrid, 1958.

————. *Persiles y Sigismunda,* ed. Rodolfo Schevill and Adolfo Bonilla. 2 vols. Madrid, 1914.

————. *Persiles y Sigismunda,* ed. Juan B. Avalle-Arce. Madrid, 1969.

Chaucer, Geoffrey. *The Complete Works,* ed. W. W. Skeat. IV. Oxford, 1940.

Cholières, Nicolas de. *Œuvres de Cholières,* ed. E. Tricotel. N.p., 1879.

Chrysostom, St. *In Matthaeum Homiliae. PG,* LVII-LVIII.

Cosmas Indicopleustes. *The Christian Topography,* ed. E. O. Winstedt. Cambridge, 1909.

Dante Alighieri. *The Divine Comedy,* ed. with trans. John Sinclair. 3 vols. New York, 1961.

Deguileville, Guillaume de. *The Pilgrimage of the Life of Man,* trans. John Lydgate. London, 1889.

Discourse of the Terrestrial Paradise, aiming at a more probable discovery of the true situation of that happy place of our first parents habitation. Printed by James Fletcher. London, 1666.

Ebreo, Leone. *Dialoghi d'Amore,* ed. S. Caramella. Bari, 1929.

Erasmo, Desiderio. *Obras escogidas,* ed. Lorenzo Riber. Madrid, 1956.

Etherie. *Journal de voyage,* ed. with trans. Helene Petre. Paris, 1948.

Flamenca. In *Les Troubadours,* eds. René Lavaud and René Nelli. N.p., n.d.

Fletcher, John. *The Pilgrim,* ed. with alterations John Dryden. Philadelphia, 1811.

Fulcher of Chartres. *Historia Hierosolymitana. PL,* CLV, 821-942.

Góngora, Luis de. *Las soledades,* ed. Dámaso Alonso. Madrid, 1956.

Gracián, Baltasar. *El criticón,* ed. M. Romera-Navarro. 3 vols. Philadelphia, 1940.

Gracián, Jerónimo de. *La peregrinación de Anastasio.* Barcelona, 1966.

Greg, W. W., ed. *Everyman.* Vaduz, 1963.

Grimmelshausen, Johann Jakob Christoffel von. *Der abentheuerliche Simplicius Simplicissimus,* ed. Felix Bobertag. 2 vols. Berlin, 1882-1883.

Hagenmeyer, Heinrich, ed. Gesta Francorum et aliorum Hierosolymitorum. Heidelberg, 1890.

Heliodorus. *Heliodori Aethiopica,* ed. Aristides Colonna. *Scriptores Graeci et Latini.* Roma, 1938.

————. *Historia di Heliodoro delle cose Ethiopiche,* trans. into Italian by Leonardo Glinci. Venezia, 1586.

————. *Historia Etiópica de los amores de Teágenes y Cariclea,* trans. into Spanish by Fernando de Mena; ed. Francisco López Estrada. Madrid, 1954.

Henricus Salteriensis. *Tractatus de Purgatorio Sancti Patrici*. PL, CLXXX, 975-1004.

Henricus, S. R. *Tractatus de peregrinante civitate Dei*. PL, CCIV, 251-402.

História Trágico-Marítima, compiled by Bernardo Gómes de Brito. Lisboa, 1905.

Homer. *The Odyssey*, ed. with trans. A. T. Murray. 2 vols. London, 1930.

Irving, Washington. *The Alhambra*. New York, 1884.

Jacopo da Voragine. *Leggenda aurea*, ed. Arrigo Levasti. 3 vols. Firenze, 1924-1925.

Kempis, Thomas à. *De Imitatione Christi Libri Quattuor*, ed. J. Valart. Paris, 1773.

Krauss, Carl von, ed. *Deutsche Liederdichter des 13. Jahrhunderts*. 2 vols. Tübingen, 1952.

Langland, William. *The Vision of William Concerning Piers the Plowman*, ed. W. W. Skeat. London, 1923.

Las Casas, Bartolomé de. *Historia de las Indias*. BAE, XCV.

Le Reverend, Julio, ed. *Cartas de relación de la conquista de América*. 2 vols. Mexico, 1945.

Leyen, Friedrich von der, ed. *Deutsche Dichtung des Mittelalters*. Frankfurt, 1962.

Lloyd, Lodovico. *The Marrow of History or, the Pilgrimage of Kings and Princes*. London, 1653.

Lorris, Guillaume de. *Le Roman de la Rose*, ed. Francisque Michel. 2 vols. Paris, 1864.

Luna, H. de. *Segunda parte de Lazarillo de Tormes*. BAE, III.

Machado de Silva, Felix. "*Tercera parte de Guzmán de Alfarache*," ed. Gerhard Moldenhauer. RH, LXIX (1927).

Maundeville, Sir John. *The Voiage and Travaile*, ed. J. D. Halliwell. London, 1883.

Mendes Pinto, Fernão. *Peregrinação*, ed. A. Casais Monteiro. 2 vols. Lisboa, 1962.

Menéndez y Pelayo, Marcelino. *Orígenes de la novela*. Buenos Aires, 1943.

Meyer, Hans E., ed. *Das Itinerarium peregrinorum*. In *Schriften der Monumenta Germaniae historica*. XVIII. Stuttgart, 1962.

Montaigne, Michel de. *Œuvres complètes*, ed. A. Armingaud. I. Paris, 1924.

Montemayor, Jorge de. *Los siete libros de la Diana*, ed. Francisco López Estrada. *Clásicos Castellanos*, Vol. 127. Madrid, 1967.

Ovidius Naso. *Metamorphoses*, with trans. by Frank J. Miller. London, 1925.

Petrarca, Francesco. *Rime*, ed. Siro Attilo Nulli. Milano, 1956.

Pinto, Hector. *Imagen de la vida cristiana*, ed. Edward Glaser. Barcelona, 1967.

Polo, Gil. *La Diana enamorada*, ed. Rafael Ferreres. *Clásicos Castellanos*, Vol. 135. Madrid, 1953.

Ponchiroli, Daniele, ed. *Lirici del Cinquecento*. Torino, 1958.

Porto, Luigi da. *Novella novamente ritrovata d'un Innamorato: Il quale successe in Verona nel tempo del Signor Bartholomeo de la Scala: Historia Iocundissima*, ed. Maurice Jonas. London, 1921.

Purchas, Samuel. *Purchas His Pilgrimes*. 14 vols. Glasgow, 1905.

Quevedo, Francisco de. *El buscón*, ed. Américo Castro. *Clásicos Castellanos*, Vol. 5, Madrid, 1960.

Rabelais, François. *Œuvres complètes,* ed. Jean Plattard. Paris, 1929.
Ribeiro, Bernardim. *Obras completas.* I. Lisboa, 1949.
Rochegude, H. P. de, ed. *Le Parnasse occitanien.* Toulouse, 1819.
Rodrigues Lobo, Francisco. *Corte na aldea* & *obras pastoras.* Lisboa, 1722.
Rojas, Fernando de. *Tragicomedia de Calixto y Melibea,* ed. M. Criado de Val and G. D. Trotter. Madrid, 1965.
Rose, Martial, ed. *The Wakefield Mystery Plays.* London, 1961.
Sannazaro, Jacopo. *Opere,* ed. Enrico Carrara. Torino, 1952.
Schiller, Friedrich. *Gesammelte Werke.* I. Berlin, 1955.
Schurhammer, G. and J. Wicki, ed. *Epistolae S. Francisci aliqui eius scripta.* I. Roma, 1944.
Selmer, Carl, ed. *Navigatio Sancti Brendani abbatis.* In *Publications in Medieval Studies.* Notre Dame, Ind., 1959.
Shafer, R., ed. *From Beowulf to Thomas Hardy.* 2 vols. New York, 1939.
Shakespeare, William. *The Oxford Shakespeare,* ed. W. J. Craig. New York, 1936.
Spenser, Edmund. *The Works,* ed. John Todd. London, 1877.
Staveren, Augustinus van. *Auctores Mythographi Latini.* Amstelaed, 1742.
Tasso, Torquato. *La Gerusalemme liberata,* ed. Giovanni Getto. Brescia, 1960.
———. *Opere,* ed. Bruno Maier. I. Milano, 1963.
Timoneda, Juan de. *Aucto del Castillo de Emaus,* ed. Mildred Edith Johnson. In *University of Iowa Studies in Spanish Language and Literature.* IV. Iowa City, 1933. 15-42.
Vega, Garcilaso de la. *Obras completas,* ed. Elias L. Rivers. Madrid, 1964.
Vega Carpio, Lope de. *La Arcadia. BAE,* XXXVIII.
———. *Obras escogidas,* ed F. C. Sáinz de Robles. 3 vols. Madrid, 1946.
———. *El peregrino en su patria.* In *Colección de las obras sueltas.* V. Madrid, 1776.
La vida de Lazarillo de Tormes, ed. Julio Cejador y Frauca. *Clásicos Castellanos,* Vol. 25. Madrid, 1926.
Wagner, Richard. *Dramatische Werke.* I. Ed. Karl Reuschel. Leipzig, 1918.
Wilde, Oscar. *The Picture of Dorian Gray.* New York, 1964.

Secondary sources

Alonso, Amado. "Don Quijote no asceta, pero ejemplar y cristiano," *NRFH,* II (1948), 333-359.
Alonso, Dámaso. *Poesía de la Edad Media y poesía de tipo tradicional.* Buenos Aires, 1942.
Alphandéry, Paul. *La Chrétienté et l'idée de la croisade.* Paris, 1954.
Alter, Robert. *Rogue's Progress: Studies in the Picaresque Novel.* Cambridge, 1964.
Atkinson, W. C. "The Enigma of the *Persiles,*" *BSS,* XXIV (1947), 242-253.
Avalle-Arce, Juan B. *La novela pastoril española.* Madrid, 1959.
———. "El poeta en su poema," *Revista de Occidente,* XCV (1971), 152-171.
Bertini, Giovanni M. "L'*Orlando Furioso* e l'Inquisizione Spagnuola," *Convivium,* VII (1935), 540-550.
Bishop, Morris. *Petrarch and His World* Bloomington, Indiana, 1963.
Blackstone, Bernard. *The Lost Travellers.* London, 1962.
Brand, C. P. *Torquato Tasso.* Cambridge, 1965.

Campenhausen, Hans von. *Die Asketische Heimatlosigkeit im altkirchlichen und frühmittelalterlichen Mönchtum.* Tübingen, 1930.

Cassirer, Ernst. *The Individual and the Cosmos in Renaissance Philosophy,* trans. Mario Domandi. New York, 1964.

Castiglione, Baldessar. *Il Libro del corteggiano,* ed. Michele Scherillo. Milano, 1928.

Castro, Américo. *El pensamiento de Cervantes.* Madrid, 1925.

Chew, Samuel C. *The Pilgrimage of Life.* New Haven and London, 1962.

Cohen, Gustave. *La Poésie en France au Moyen Age.* Paris, 1952.

Curtius, Ernst Robert. *European Literature and the Latin Middle Ages,* trans. Willard R. Trask. New York, 1963.

Dodds, Madelaine Hope and Ruth Dodds. *The Pilgrimage of Grace 1536-37 and the Exeter Conspiracy 1538.* 2 vols. Cambridge, 1915.

Durling, Robert M. *The Figure of the Poet in Renaissance Epic.* Cambridge, Mass., 1965.

Elbers, Winfried. *Das deutsche Soldatenlied im 1. Weltkrieg und seine publizistische Bedeutung.* Essen, 1963.

Erdmann, Carl. *Die Entstehung des Kreuzzugsgedankens.* Stuttgart, 1955.

Feijoo, Benito J. *Peregrinaciones sagradas y romerías. BAE,* CXLII, 51-56.

Friedrich, Carl J. *The Age of the Baroque.* New York, 1965.

Fuhrmann, Joseph P. *Irish Medieval Monasteries on the Continent.* Washington, 1927.

Galpin, Stanley Leman. "On the Sources of Guillaume de Deguileville's Pèlerinage de l'ame," *PMLA,* XXV (1910), 275-308.

Gerhardt, Mia Irene. *La Pastorale.* Assen, 1950.

Giamatti, A. Bartlett. *The Earthly Paradise and the Renaissance Epic.* Princeton, 1966.

Gougaud, Dom Louis. *Devotional and Ascetic Practices in the Middle Ages,* trans. G. C. Bateman. London, 1927.

―――. *Gaelic Pioneers of Christianity,* trans. Victory Collins. Dublin, 1923.

Green, Otis H. *Spain and the Western Tradition.* 4 vols. Madison, 1963-1966.

Hafter, Monroe Z. *Gracián and Perfection: Spanish Moralists of the Seventeenth Century.* Cambridge, Mass., 1966.

Harnack, Adolf. *Militia Christi. Die christliche Religion und der Soldatenstand in den ersten drei Jahrhunderten.* Tübingen, 1905.

Hatzfeld, Helmut. "Don Quijote asceta?" *NRFH,* II (1948), 57-70.

―――. *El "Quijote" como obra de arte del lenguage.* Madrid, 1949.

―――. *Estudios sobre el barroco.* Madrid, 1964.

Heath, Sidney. *In the Steps of the Pilgrims.* New York, 1951.

Heer, Friedrich. *The Medieval World,* trans. Janet Sondheimer. New York, 1962.

Herrmann, Paul. *Conquest by Man.* London, 1954.

Highet, Gilbert. *The Classical Tradition.* New York, 1961.

Hubatsch, Walter. *Quellen zur Geschichte des Deutschen Ordens.* Göttingen, 1954.

Huizinga, Johan. *The Waning of the Middle Ages.* New York, 1954.

Jeanroy, Alfred. *La Poésie lyrique des troubadours.* 2 vols. Toulouse, 1958.

Knauer, G. N. "Peregrinatio Animae," *Hermes,* LXXXV (1957), 216 ff.

Kötting, B. *Peregrinatio religiosa: Wallfahrten in der alten Kirche.* Regensburg, 1950.

Lambin, Georges. "Passionate Pilgrims," *Etudes Anglaises* XVII (1964), 457-463.

Lardner, Gerhart. *"Homo viator:* Medieval Ideas on Alienation and Order," *Speculum,* XLII (1967), 233-251.

Lattimore, Richard. *Themes in Greek and Latin Epitaphs.* In *Illinois Studies in Language and Literature.* XXVII. Urbana, 1942.

Leclercq, Jean. "Monachisme et pérégrination du IXᵉ au XIIᵉ siècle," *Studia Monastica,* III (1961), 33-52.

Lecoy, Felix. *Récherches sur le Libro de buen amor.* Paris, 1938.

Leithäuser, Joachim. *Worlds Beyond the Horizon,* trans. H. Merrick. New York, 1955.

Levey, Michel. "The Real Theme of Watteau's *Embarcation for Cytheria,*" *The Burlington Magazine,* CIII (1961), 180-185.

Lewis, C. S. *The Allegory of Love.* New York, 1958.

Livermore, H. V. *A History of Portugal.* Cambridge, Mass., 1947.

López Pinciano, Alonso. *Philosophía antigua poética,* ed. Alfredo Carballo Picazo. 3 vols. Madrid, 1953.

Loyola, San Ignacio de. *Obras completas,* ed. Ignacio Iparraguirre. Madrid, 1952.

Martini, Fritz. *Deutsche Literaturgeschichte.* Stuttgart, 1961.

Moreno-Báez, Enrique. *Lección y sentido del "Guzmán de Alfarache."* Madrid, 1943.

Panofsky, Erwin. *Studies in Iconology.* New York, 1964.

Parker, Alexander A. *The Allegorical Drama of Calderón.* Oxford and London, 1943.

————. *Literature and the Delinquent.* Edinburgh, 1967.

Parry, J. H. *The Age of Reconnaissance.* New York, 1964.

Patch, Howard R. *The Other World According to Descriptions in Medieval Literature.* Cambridge, Mass., 1950.

Pitt, Don. *Pilgrim's Progress: 20th Century. The Story of Salvation Army Officership.* New York, 1950.

Predmore, Richard L. *El mundo del Quijote.* Madrid, 1958.

Rauhut, Franz. "La picaresca española en la literatura alemana," *RFH,* I (1939), 237-256.

Rein, A. *Die Europäische Ausbreitung über die Erde.* Potsdam, 1931.

Reitzenstein, Richard. *Historia Monachorum und Historia Lausiaca.* Göttingen, 1916.

Riley, E. C. *Cervantes's Theory of the Novel.* Oxford, 1962.

Roppen, Georg and Richard Sommer. *Strangers and Pilgrims.* New York, 1964.

Rougement, Denis de. *Love and the Western World,* trans. Montgomery Belgion. New York, 1966.

Sainz Rodríguez, Pedro. *Introducción a la historia de la literatura mística en España.* Madrid, 1927.

Schüttpelz, Otto. "Die Erscheinungen vor den Emmausjüngern und den Aposteln: Das Lateinische Peregrinispiel," *Germanistische Abhandlungen,* LXVII (1930), 56-161.

Spengler, Oswald. *The Decline of the West,* trans. Charles F. Atkinson; ed. Arthur Phelps. New York, 1965.

Spitzer, Leo. *Classical and Christian Ideas of World Harmony*. Baltimore, 1963.

――――. *Die Literarisierung des Lebens in Lopes "Dorotea."* Bonn, 1932.

――――. *Romanische Literaturstudien*. Tübingen, 1959.

――――. *Romanische Stil- und Literaturstudien*. 2 vols. Marburg, 1931.

――――. *Literary Masterpieces of the Western World*, ed. Francis H. Horn. Baltimore, 1953.

――――. "Zur Kunst Quevedos in seinem *Buscón*," *Archivum Romanicum*, XI (1927), 511-580.

Stanford, W. B. *The Ulysses Theme*. Oxford, 1963.

Taylor, E. W. *Nature and Art in the Renaissance*. New York, 1965.

Vilanova, Antonio. "El peregrino andante en el *Persiles* de Cervantes," *Boletín de la Real Academia de buenas letras de Barcelona*, XXII (1949), 97-159.

――――. "El peregrino de amor en las *Soledades* de Góngora," in *Estudios dedicados a Menéndez Pidal* (Madrid, 1952), III, 421-460.

Villey, Michel. *La Croisade*. Paris, 1942.

Vossler, Karl. *Lope de Vega y su tiempo*, trans. Ramón de la Serna. Madrid, 1933.

――――. *La poesía de la soledad en España*. Buenos Aires, 1946.

Wardropper, Bruce W. "The *Diana* of Montemayor: Revaluation and Interpretation," *SP*, XLVIII (1951), 126-144.

――――. "*Don Quijote*: Story or History?" *MP*, LXIII (1965), 1-11.

――――. *Historia de la poesía lírica a lo divino*. Madrid, 1958.

――――. *Introducción al teatro religioso del Siglo de Oro*. Madrid, 1953.

――――. "El trastorno de la moral en el *Lazarillo*," *NRFH*, XV (1961), 441-447.

Wright, J. K. *The Geographical Lore of the Time of the Crusades*. New York, 1965.

INDEX